Television,

a memoir

Also by Karen Brennan

Poetry

Here on Earth
The Real Enough World
little dark

Fiction

Wild Desire
The Garden in Which I Walk
Monsters

Memoir

Being with Rachel

Television, a memoir

Karen Brennan

Four Way Books

Tribeca

To Kira and Hannah,

Beloveds

Library of Congress Cataloging-in-Publication Data

Names: Brennan, Karen, 1941- author.
Title: Television, a memoir / Karen Brennan.
Description: Tribeca : Four Way Books, [2022]
Identifiers: LCCN 2021045625 (print) | LCCN 2021045626 (ebook)
ISBN 9781954245075 (trade paperback) | ISBN 9781954245167 (epub)
Subjects: LCSH: Brennan, Karen, 1941- | Poets, American--20th century--Biography. | LCGFT: Autobiographies.
Classification: LCC PS3552.R378 Z46 2022 (print) | LCC PS3552.R378 (ebook) | DDC 811/.54 [B]--dc23/eng/20211018
LC record available at https://lccn.loc.gov/2021045625
LC ebook record available at https://lccn.loc.gov/2021045626

Four Way Books is a not-for-profit literary press. We are grateful for the assistance we receive from individual donors, public arts agencies, and private foundations including the NEA, NEA Cares, Literary Arts Emergency Fund, and the New York State Council on the Arts, a state agency.

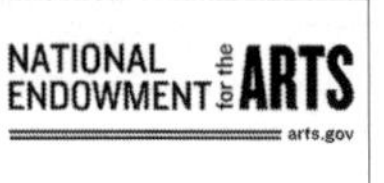

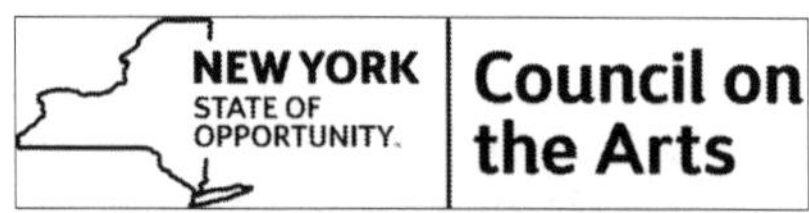

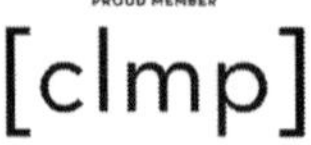

We are a proud member of the Community of Literary Magazines and Presses.

Contents

*

Word/mist, word/mist: thus it was with me.
And yet, my silence was never total—

Louise Glück

TELEVISION

The first television in our neighborhood belonged to the O'Neils who lived in the big brown house across the street. Lodged in a shiny console, possibly Bakelite, and flanked by a weird assortment of knobs, it reminded me of my doll's oven.

That night, our family was among those neighbors who trooped across the street to witness the contraption for the first time. The evening air shifted restlessly, as if marking the end of a more predictable era—otherwise, the neighborhood was as quiet as it usually was in those days, the houses in deep shadow except for the yellow halos coming from lamps set upon tables covered with family photographs in silver frames. Nowadays when you look in windows of houses in the evening you usually see the blue flickering lights of the TV, but back then the windows glowed more steadily and people read books or washed the dishes or darned socks, as my mother actually did, in the evenings. We had a Victrola, as it was then called, and sometimes we listened to music, but not very often since my mother preferred classical and did not like to burden us with her taste.

About fifteen of us gathered in the front room of the O'Neils' big house, a sort of square hallway beneath the staircase, where the TV had been installed on a table. A few chairs were brought around, but most of us stood on the green wall-to-wall carpeting, craning our necks around those in front of us, ready for whatever it was.

I have no idea what we saw, what black-and-white image blinked stupidly across the screen and I was not impressed. I was a self-absorbed child and the picture was hard to see, not pleasurable, and thus of no concern to me. To everyone else it had been a shock (I recall my mother shrieking) like seeing a chair fly across the room or a dish of apples suddenly begin to cough.

POLIO

When disease visited our family, casting its brutal shadow, our days became marked by whispers followed by long nervous silences, as though someone had mentioned the unmentionable and then felt guilty about it. It was infectious. I was ashamed, too.

There was a sick brother, whisked away in a blue blanket. My mother wore a red jacket, my father a tan raincoat; the baby was invisible beneath the blanket. A tableau, they stood by the front door, the door slightly ajar, in the act of leaving in the rain. They stayed there a long time, motionless, posing for my memory of them.

HOME

I grew up in a town whose streets were names for trees, a famed bedroom community, home to the newly rich commuter, yet I had roots there. Both of my parents were raised in this town and two sets of grandparents lived nearby for all of our childhoods, the paternal set on Oak Avenue and the maternal on Magnolia, though I was never sure if those squat magnolia shrubs should be counted as real trees.

We lived on Willow. There were no willows on our street, only a gigantic weeping beech in our neighbor's yard. We used to play in the cave formed by its drooping branches, which was unusually capacious and filled with a purple light.

Of our two sets of grandparents, I spent more time with my mother's parents. They lived in a mansion with many servants and needlepoint bell chords used to summon them. Their yard contained a big oak tree, which is still there, even though the house has changed hands several times since then. It was under the oak that the shiny barbeque, hauled out from the garage on special occasions, was situated, and where the chauffer Jack used to grill chicken. These occasions my grandmother called "picnics," a feature of which was her special German Potato Salad: potatoes, bacon, parsley and a warm vinaigrette, ingredients assembled beforehand by the kitchen staff. My grandmother's job was to toss it all together and then to call it her Special German Potato Salad.

There were always the flies to contend with, so little white nets on metal armatures were placed over the food—the potato salad, the string beans from the garden, the chicken and thin slices of a frosted lemon cake. I swung back and forth on one of the swinging couches of that era, picking at my chicken, waiting for the cake.

A fishpond adorned with a 19th-century bronze mermaid, soulfully arranged on a pedestal, presided over the unnaturally large goldfish. I used to let them slither through the tunnels I made with my fingers, beneath the shimmering reflection of my big face looking down. I liked the look of certain things: the goldfish who were not gold but a neon orange and the narrow, pebbled pathways that wove among the rose gardens, the pebbles tiny, white and uniform, more like pearls than pebbles. I used to wonder if they'd been specially created for these pathways.

Everything at those grandparents was "specially" done; the food was specially ordered or grown, the table roses came from a special place, my grandmother had her clothes made specially for her at a dressmaker's in New York City. It was two flights up in an old brownstone building, a small and slightly dingy apartment, where we'd be greeted by a flock of busy women, all with pins in their mouths and yellow measuring tapes draped around their shoulders. In the future, I would get my trousseau there.

I wasn't interested in my appearance and when I looked in the mirror, I felt that the face I beheld was not my own. Why this face and no other? I remember wondering. In place of thinking, I dwelled in wondering—not bafflement exactly, but surprise that this or that would be such and such a way, combined with a kind of anxious curiosity. I hoped all things would be revealed to me, sooner or later. In retrospect, I can see that my life was marked by my anxiety, and in order to contain it, I kept myself calm. This is the condition of the powerless.

There were always a lot of rules in the Willow house as well as the Magnolia house. Mealtimes were regimented, likewise bedtimes and playtimes. One was forbidden to venture into certain rooms, sit on certain chairs, and touch certain objects. Food also was curtailed—no candy, no eating between meals, don't overload your plate, you can always have seconds, only one cookie, don't gulp your milk, hand on your lap over your napkin, don't talk. Dinnertime at the Willow house crackled with tension since our father had a temper and was apt to leap up after shouting at one of us and hurl his napkin on his plate and storm out of the room. I don't remember enjoying food in that house, sitting with my siblings and parents, my mother clearing her throat nervously as she struggled with her fork and napkin (she was a "cripple," which was her word for herself), my father given to those sharp outbursts that made us startle.

The Magnolia dinners were also bound by the rules of etiquette, but the rituals were lovely and sensual, matters of aesthetics rather than protocol. There are few things in my childhood that gave me as much pleasure as dipping my fingertips into the little crystal fingerbowl between courses and blotting my moistened fingers into the napkin on my lap and shifting the bowl with its doily to the left of my plate. The tiny individual salt dishes with their silver spoons are a close second—

Likewise, I loved my dollhouse, an impressive structure that sprawled over a square bridge table. The little rooms full of little things—a blue table for the breakfast room and upholstered chairs in the dining room and a set of miniscule glasses with stripes on them and glass cocktail stirrers as thin as needles. The china figures of mother, father, baby, big and little sisters composed the perfect family, perfectly expressionless in their felt outfits. The maid who wore a black apron trimmed with lace and a crumb-sized white cap leaned eternally against the stove.

If only, like Alice, I could drink a potion and shrink down and lounge on the silk sofa, the tiny newspaper in my hands. And there I'd be.

SHAME

When I was six, I tortured a girl. We ordered her to stand against a tree in her own backyard while we waved dog shit in front of her face, screaming at her to smell and eat. The girl had a soft pale face with eyes that were almost transparent. I remember her gazing at us with tears in her eyes and the horrible thrill that scudded through my body. Along with others I screamed and waved my own stick with its glob of dog shit. I had not been a popular child and I suppose the thrill was just as much at being invited to participate with the gang of girls that usually excluded me.

The girl who had been our neighbor had light brown hair. Her fingers were red, her fingernails bitten. It's all lodged in memory—the tree with its copper, spoon-shaped leaves, the cold smell of the air, the white sky. And her name, like yesterday, each flaming syllable.

MILTOWN

My mother took a Miltown every morning, which is one of the reasons I decided to be a slob. My mother: preternaturally neat. I thought—still think—the Miltown had something to do with it. She swallowed a Miltown with her morning coffee and felt tranquil for the rest of the day, even though her life had basically no meaning apart from being a housewife.

To be clear, my mother did not perform the duties of a housewife. She employed others to do that. She was paralyzed as a result of polio at the age of 33 and was confined to a wheelchair for most of her 89 years. Being confined to a wheelchair was no picnic and I suppose the Miltown helped get her through the day, which in any case was dull and uneventful, except for the occasional employee who stole or didn't follow her precise instructions about the preparation of her morning egg.

After polio, she'd become finicky, anxious, OCD before that term was commonplace. Her drawers were organized as if for photo shoots. Rubber bands end to end in a small blue box. A jar of multi-colored thumbtacks, a row of pencils, perfectly sharpened, like daggers.

My mother who studied modern dance with Martha Graham, who traveled to Europe on ocean liners, who'd been wooed by Mr. Universe, danced with a Prince, and owned hundreds of pairs of shoes.

AFTER LACAN

I discovered my inner life when staring at my thumb. My mother had covered it with a red awful-tasting medicine so I would not suck it. I was still in a crib and I remember a room in shadow and a door leading to another, brighter room. My mother's filmy peignoir floated out from her body as she moved. Transparent, it caught the objects of the brighter room, even as it muted their brightness. She stood in the entry, the portal between one room and another and watched me in my crib, having just soaked my thumb in the bitter medicine. I had adored sucking my thumb. Now that it was no longer available, a dazzling chasm opened within me, and I saw myself seeing myself—me, myself, both of us as one—grieving.

MIRROR

My mother, renowned for her beauty, at her dressing table, leaning into her mirror image, applying cake mascara with the tiniest of brushes. I stood behind the reflection she studied so critically, a furrow creasing her brow, thus two of us framed in the mirror's silvered square: a foreground and a background.

Her hair was a color referred to as chestnut; her lips were Paint-the-Town-Red, courtesy of Revlon. In her closet, numerous pairs of shoes on shelves. Rows of mules. The green mules, I recall, being fuzzy and open-toed. The pink were satin with a flower.

I stood there, at one remove, my obedient expression just behind my mother's cloud of hair, her shoulder erasing my overalls. I thought of the evil queen in the story.

Mirror Mirror on the Wall, I whispered.

Sunlight was streaming through the window in the room,

streaming through the venetian blinds, casting long bright rectangles on the carpeting.

My mother was the fairest, I assured her. I knew none as fair as she, I said.

BAM ZOOM

My father's voice, boiling with testosterone and rage, frightened us. He was the king of our castle. He sat at the end of the table, a meat-and-potatoes guy, shouting orders. On holidays, he toasted himself, raising his glass of Dewar's on the rocks above the heads of his four children and his disabled wife. *Not many guys would stick around in a situation like this,* he'd tell us. *They would have packed it in years ago.*

Jackie Gleason, sweeping the air with his fist: *Just be a little careful, Alice, a little careful. The life you save may be your own.*

WILLOW

I've already told you that we lived on a street called Willow after the trees that never grew there. Perhaps they had grown there once in a dream, how would I know. The beech in the neighbor's yard wept. We made a house beneath its yellow tears. We lived in the house for a few years, my sister and I. We drank tea and ate sweets from the tiny scoops of acorns. When winter came, we huddled together. We called to the spirits but when they came, they frightened us—all teeth and waving arms, clawed fingers, monstrous like our nightmares. Still, we managed to escape. Our spells enchanted our enemies, made them stupid and slow, and we flew to the highest branches, crouching behind a bird's nest.

We can still do this, when called upon. We can still live wherever we want. We can still escape. Even as the house grows tight around us, we remind ourselves. Even as the path becomes a tightrope and we are too exhausted to move.

ALLEGORY

For a year or so I lived in a teacup. I had become very small (it might have been the inoculations) and before I knew it, there I was. I was comfortable enough. I was given little crumbs as befitted my stature, but various things became dangerous. A thumb could kill me, for example. And don't let us consider the ants. Also, I was lonely. I never went anywhere, never met anyone. It was very white in there, very glary. My mother's voice was like a symphony of violins that lifted me and affirmed my belief in angels. In contrast, my father's voice was a furious explosion, tossing me from side to side and hurting my head. Because my own voice had become tiny and soft, no one, not even the angelic orders, could hear me when I cried out.

BROWN

The brown of our neighbor's house is what distinguished it for me. It was a rambling, many-roofed house, but the brown, like the oxfords I had to wear to Catholic boarding school, is what stood out, even more than the gracious wrap-around porch and the gnarly apple tree in the front yard that we would climb up and into (though it is a mistake to think of me as one of the apple-tree gang because I was usually outside the group, either confined by my mother to the other side of the street in a party dress or not agile or brave enough to climb a tree).

O was my friend in that house and she had the kind of power that only a child can wield, one composed of a ruthless indifference to the adoration of her peers. On one of the few occasions she came to my house for an afternoon, my mother fed her strawberries and cream, which she threw up on our rug, an act that meant more to me than it should have, and I ladled it with my humiliation and tucked it into the underwear drawer of my shame.

When permitted, I went to her house and tried to climb the tree or play with other neighborhood kids, the games consisting of exploratory sex probes that were tremendously exciting to me, as well as various dance routines we invented for our girl club, The Five Friendly Fairies. I don't know from whence we drew that alliterative name, but we assumed all the earmarks of a professional club, with a president, vice president, secretary, treasurer and so on. In other words, four of us assuming some office or other and one of us—me—assuming the role of dues-paying member.

I can still see myself sitting on the dirt floor of our clubhouse, proffering my dime and answering "here" when the fairy roll was called.

ANGELS

My mother believed in angels, especially in her guardian angel who was called Bernard. Bernard appeared to her at crucial moments in her life and reassured her. I have always pictured Bernard as wearing flowing robes and having beautifully articulated golden wings. My image of Bernard must have come from Renaissance paintings, such as those by Caravaggio, just as our idea of paradise and hell come from Milton's *Paradise Lost*. There is no need to read Milton or to visit the Ufizzi because all those ideas and images have been absorbed into our cultural DNA and have become clichés. But there is a difference, my mother would contend, between the appearance of a real angel like Bernard and the beautiful representation of an angel by Caravaggio. What is the difference, exactly? I wondered.

MIRACLES

I went to the garden and collected rocks. These I arranged into patterns, spirals and lines, whorls inside of other whorls, little pathways to the feet of trees.

What did I think about then? The world was a blur. The world had unfastened itself and lost its clear edges. I dug in the yard with a silver spoon, then got in trouble. Once I buried my gold ring. I had a notion of China—digging so far I would arrive there. An upside-down world, I reasoned, my ring waiting on the surface.

I sat on a rock overlooking Long Island Sound and watched the triangular sails of the boats against the horizon. The horizon was a miracle, flat and not flat, and a miracle that inside those tiny boats were tiny people having conversations and yet not. The discrepancy was a miracle. Here and there was a miracle.

I was sent away to live with my kind and prosperous grandparents. On the red patterned sofa in the library, my grandmother held my hand. Grandfather fiddled with the dial on the old wooden radio.

I listened to the stock market quotations and the news. We ate breakfast in the library on a card table covered with a lacey white cloth. The maid, Rose, came with a big tray, the soft-boiled eggs still in their shells.

I prayed our mother would walk again, but that didn't happen. After a while, I felt that even the air I occupied would be better employed elsewhere. I got through each day, but it was drudgery. Today, sometimes, I get a glimmer of that drudgery, the dull labor of hauling myself through time. I find myself counting the minutes. But counting the minutes to what?

PINK DESK

My mother kept stamps in a round wooden box which I've inherited—its circumference is decorated with ghosts of flowers, very faded, and on the lid, a green fish with an elaborate tail and some words I can't read.

Wheelchaired in front of her pink desk, she slid the stamps as needed through the vertical slot at the tiny box's edge, licked and affixed them to the envelopes of her thank-you notes with her one good hand.

My mother had only one good hand, as she put it, as we all put it. The other one rested placidly in her lap, the ovals of her nails pale and immaculate. With her bad, nondominant hand, her penmanship was backward glancing and arched like so many entryways to so many sweeping meadows she'd never get to dance through.

Most days we forgot about our mother's disability, although it made us odd. We went on growing up, shouting and disobeying and laughing and fighting while my mother sat at the pink desk, busy with her interminable gratitude.

You'd think I would have learned from this, but it annoyed me, the writing of thank yous so absurd—those painstaking sentences full of weary clichés. Waste of time!

Nice days, she sat outside, with a crossword, near the lilacs and their heart-shaped leaves and the neighbors' privet hedge.

Winters, she watched the soaps or cooking shows and read Ruskin and Thomas Carlyle and the histories of England and Spain. She spoke French to the maid. She had her hair done once a week; an invisible spiderweb net enclosed her glossed bouffant for the next seven days.

There was a time, pre-polio, that she changed the lightbulbs. She made hollandaise sauce. She drove us to school.

Afterwards, she suffered quietly like the *mater dolorosa*, eyes downcast, and wrote her thank yous despite us.

I REMEMBER MAMA

For the evening's compulsory TV watching, we are gathered in the den, I on the floor, slumped against a chair, wondering what it is I am supposed to feel about this gathering of Norwegian immigrants in 1910 San Francisco who do not correspond in any way to my middle-class, not-so-amiable family. Mama's life of drudgery is unappealing as is the horribly pigtailed Dagmar with her coy Shirley Temple affectations. Mama herself, played by Peggy Wood, an American actress who had perfected a Scandinavian accent, bustles around contentedly in a checked apron that, in an effort to emulate the poor's lack of discernment, willfully clashes with her floral blouse. She makes the beds, plans the suppers, darns the socks, and sews the buttons; washes dishes, scrubs floors, dusts knick-knacks and consumes caffeine. Indeed, at the outset of every show she scoops coffee from a can of Maxwell House, the show's proud sponsor, into a vintage coffeepot, a clone of which is now available on eBay for $72.50. This item was possessed by our own mother who never used it. When she bequeathed it to me, it burnt to death on my stove.

BOMB SCARES

If you are old, you will remember bomb scares. A siren went off and we hid beneath our desks, arms folded protectively over our heads. Picture our village: houses and cars and grocery stores whirling and tossing in the mushroom cloud, and we school children under our desks, miraculously preserved. Ridiculous, but we did as we were told.

One day, I brought a trick lipstick to class. You loaded the lipstick with a cap from a toy pistol and when it was opened by a person, it would "explode." In class, a boy I liked opened the lipstick I'd deliberately dropped on the floor near his foot. I hid under my desk and waited for the world to end.

HAPPY DAYS

Whoa! said the Fonz, my favorite character. The Fonz loved Pinky, Pinky with her pre-punk tiny-skirted glamour, Yamaha motorcycle off to the demolition derby, fuck you boys. Not so testosterone fueled as what's-his-name or as saintly as the redhead, Fonzy was the perfect male. In the same way, I liked Jughead from the Archie Comics—not handsome, not noble, but funny, even funny looking. In real life, a guy called Roger Something who never noticed me though I yearned for him. Awkward, clunky, big-nosed Roger Something who wore a grey sweatshirt day and night and wasn't good at baseball.

RESISTANCE

Growing up we had a mute bird called Paulie with whom my mother fell in love. More than anything, she wanted Paulie to talk and she devoted hours to his lessons, cajoling him with a soft, intimate, unfamiliar voice, the voice of a lover. I can still see her, wheelchair pulled up to the cage, trying to make Paulie say *Paulie*. Paulie, she supposed, was a male—though how she supposed this is a mystery—and his name was the male version of *Polly*.

My mother was clever when it came to words. *Le bon mot*, she said of her gift. But Paulie would not speak; Paulie would not even try. He went on his indifferent way, eating the seeds and water provided, shitting tiny black and white turds on the paper lining of his cage.

I did not love Paulie. In his aluminum cage rattling on a sideboard in our dining room, with his lurid blue wings and his beady, immovable eyes, he seemed more toy than bird. The only thing that might have persuaded me of Paulie's reality was his refusal to speak, as the instructions had promised. Because I knew that trick.

POSTURE

I have a lot of stories to tell about the good old days. One of them may involve my child's pediatrician asking if I knew how to take a baby's temperature. I was on Public Assistance at the time and he assumed, well you know, et cetera and so forth (that I knew nothing).

Another was the time a friend of my father's felt me up in the back seat of our car. Mom and Dad sat in front, heads frozen ahead as I quietly struggled and gasped. I was 15. The friend was the CEO of an important blue-chip company. He had enormous hands with perfectly groomed fingernails. *Oh baby, come here, baby*, he kept saying.

I kept a low profile after that, even though I enjoyed wearing lipstick.

The pediatrician said, *show me*. And the worst is that I did, turning my burning infant onto her stomach and plunging the rectal thermometer into her screaming self. You should be a nurse, my father used to say. Or an airline stewardess, which is what they were called then. Comb your hair, he said. You'd be a good stewardess. My mother said, you should join a commune. That was the best idea, though I didn't do it.

The CEO who felt me up was very fond of me. He is very fond of you, my father said more than once, approvingly. It is better to be on Public Assistance than to take money from one's parents. Though it is better to have rich, oblivious parents than no parents at all, I reasoned, perhaps erroneously.

They used to say, she has a good imagination, too bad about her inferiority complex. My mother often suggested a nice pin. My father told me to stand up straight and close my mouth. This presented an unattractive picture of myself to my good imagination.

JOB

My first job was as a volunteer nurse's aide at New Rochelle hospital. My father had volunteered me. He thought if I learned some nursing skills I would be of use to my afflicted mother. It was small consolation that I got to wear a white uniform. I also wore white stockings and white shoes, like a real nurse. But no hat. I was 12.

It was, of course, summer. I rode the bus to the hospital three days a week, taking a window seat, feeling a little put-out at the prospect of the day ahead, even as I watched the boring sights of the Boston Post Road glide by. Gas stations and diners. Telephone poles and telephone booths. It was a long time ago.

I should add that I had no desire to be a nurse, that nothing about that occupation appealed to me in any way and after spending a summer emptying bedpans and holding patients for shots and arranging flowers, I was more repelled than ever.

Among the things I learned as a nurses' aide included making hospital corners on hospital beds, which would be critiqued by a melancholy nurse called Mrs. Angelini. Mrs. Angelini wore a gold crucifix on a chain that rested on her starched bosom and she was always muttering *Mother of God* while rolling her eyes heavenward. She would have us remake any beds that did not have properly folded corners. We should have been able to bounce a quarter on the beds, though none of us had quarters to bounce. We were unpaid volunteers.

It cost 15 cents to ride the bus and once, having only a dime, I pretended to lose a nickel between the seats. I made a big fuss and actually managed to bring tears to my own eyes until one of the passengers handed me the requisite change. That's how long ago it was. It cost 15 cents to ride the bus.

Once a dead man spoke to us. He said, Good morning girls, and we said, Good morning Mr. Whatever-His-Name-Was. That can't be, said Mrs. Angelini. Her blue eyes regarded us sorrowfully. That man is dead. No, he spoke to us, we insisted. A team of doctors and others were then summoned, and they tested the man, who was dead. You girls will never be good nurses, said Mrs. Angelini. We don't want to be nurses, I informed her. We want to be doctors or priests.

Another time, my friend and I were commanded to give an old lady a bath. My friend was 13. She was therefore in charge. When the old lady took off her clothes, we got a fit of the giggles. It was cruel. We couldn't stop our laughing. She had drooping breasts down to her thighs and big fleshy arms and a stomach that looked like a bagpipe. Now I look that way.

HAMMOCK

Coventry was our place in the country, away from the busy neighborhood of our NYC suburb. A hilly, wooded landscape with lakes, silver in the moonlight, one of which we could see from the porch where we sat with our comics on a swinging couch. There were no neighbors in sight. We had to go up a long drive to get to our Aunt May's house, she who shared the property as a distant neighbor and had only one eye and who painted one of her eyeglass lenses white to prevent the sight of the eye socket. Compared to her sister, our Nanny, Aunt May was quiet and somewhat demure, her hair like puffy balls of cotton floating around her head, signifying her saintliness.We were Catholics and our imaginations were never not fueled by stories of the saints, some of whom endured horrible tortures to save their souls. Might not Aunt May with her missing eye be among them?

These things preoccupied us, along with stories about the hermit in the woods surrounding our house and the fact that certain ants had a venom that could paralyze, not to mention the more frightening true life stories about hauntings and mysterious disappearances that were read aloud around the breakfast table from the *News of the World* and in the outhouse with its jagged moon and stars carved into the door, the giant *Guinness Book of World Records* with its weird, dreadful facts alongside the commode on a wooden bench.

The Coventry house proprietors were Nanny, our grandmother on our father's side, and Herb, her second husband, who was handy with the garden tools and could usually be found digging a hole or scooping out the pond which lay adjacent to the house. We swam in it only occasionally, having been warned of leeches. It was Herb who erected a hammock for our amusement. Strung between two fragile, skinny birch trees, it could only accommodate one medium-sized child at a time. As I lay gazing at the sky between the little round leaves, the birch trees creaked dangerously, and I daydreamed that one day I would fall and tumble into the leech-filled pond and that everyone would feel sorry for me.

At a certain point, a TV was purchased, but the only show I remember watching was Lawrence Welk. My grandmother was crazy about Lawrence Welk. The rest of us, including Herb, went along. I have a vague memory of sitting on the sleeper sofa and

Lawrence Welk crying “Bubbles, Bubbles!” in his peculiar accent, and the sinister look of the bubbles before the opening credits, silvery and aggressive, like pods from outer space, rising in a cloud from behind the orchestra, which was composed entirely of white men dressed identically to Welk in dark suits, white shirts and ties, slender, white pocket squares protruding from each lapel pocket.

GAMES

Jack kept the Cadillac limousine polished to a high sheen. Magical to me were the big electronic window that separated the front and back seats, and the intercom. We used to play with the window, to Jack's annoyance, and also with the intercom, shouting fake orders in the commanding manner of our grandmother, which amused him. To hear our voices projected through the long space of the car was as close as we got to technology in those days. The back seat was fitted with two jump seats that faced the regular back seat and the whole interior, even the ceiling, was covered in a dove-gray fabric. Like an expensive TV console, the dashboard was paneled in burled wood and spattered with silver dials and buttons. Only our grandfather rode in front with Jack so that I got the idea that the front seat was a place of privilege, which meant men. The women sat quietly in the back, swaddled and transported.

GLOVES

Boma wore soft gray gloves during our Lake Placid summer trips, wrist gloves. In the limousine she'd be wearing the gloves and holding our hands. On the way to New York City once, she held my hand in her three-quarter length beige kid glove and I didn't like the feel of it, so she took it off. She had beautiful, warm, soft hands, and ropey veins that I have inherited. When she shook her hands, the veins would disappear and I now do this for my own grandchildren, though they are possibly less amazed than I was by this phenomenon. There was less magic in the world then, fewer things to marvel at, so it didn't take much. The big boats in the harbor amazed us and the idea of Loon Lake, which we envisioned as a misty expanse echoing with the eerie sounds of the Loon, whatever they were. Loon Lake meant we were close to Lake Placid and we only ever knew it as a green and white sign on Route 1 and a romantic description our mother must have provided to keep us quiet.

COMING OF AGE

At 14, a shy teen with braces, pimples and a bad haircut, I was chosen to represent Luxembourg as a "princess" in the International Azalea Festival, which honors NATO by selecting a princess from each of the 15 NATO nations to participate in a pageant. Since princesses from Luxembourg were nonexistent and since my grandfather was an honorary consul general from that country, I was chosen. Unlike the other princesses, I only spoke English and was not a real princess.

The event took place over the course of a few weeks in Norfolk, Virginia and Washington, D.C. During this time, we princesses rode through cities on Thunderbird floats plastered with bushels of flowers and flanked on either side by southern beauty queens. It was, in general, a humiliating experience.

We attended flower shows, were photographed for newspapers, wore many different (but matching) outfits and were finally crowned by a dignitary from our respective nations—me by my grandfather during a short rendition of the Luxembourg national anthem which sounds like a polka. On that occasion, our gowns were green tulle and many petti-coated and I have no memory of the crown, except that it made me look like a goat.

Toward the end of these festivities, I was interviewed on television in the lobby of the Sheraton Hotel in D.C., my mother and grandmother situated nervously on the sidelines in their minks. The lobby was gilded and extravagantly cushioned. We princesses floated by royally, our heads held high as we emerged into the madding crowds. The hotel personnel made way for us, bowing worshipfully. We were photographed with the president. We slept on piles of mattresses, no peas beneath.

SHOE

Sonja was a quiet Finnish woman with mouse-gray hair and the smallest feet I'd ever seen on a grownup, who my parents had hired to cook. The night of the dinner party, Sonja was nowhere to be found. Not in the kitchen where a crop of white potatoes was smoking in a scorched pot, where a lump of roasting meat blackened in the oven. She was at last discovered in her bed, fully clothed, motionless as a corpse. For a stricken moment or two, there was a flurry of excited speculation among the dinner guests that she actually *had* died. She looked so little in the bed, like a child my own age. Then someone spotted the empty bottle—scotch? gin?—lying on its side like a cartoon. Her husband, a tall ghostly thin man, eventually arrived and, with great dignity, escorted her to their car. I remember she left her shoes, or one of them, because I can still picture it: a miniscule tan-colored flat, the heel worn down along an edge, like one of my doll's slippers.

NOTES FROM A VOYAGE

June 10, 1960, SS Constitution

A storm blew up shortly after [we departed] and I was sea sick. The food is delicious. Our cabin is very nice. I wore my green and white suit all day and my blue silk for cocktails and dinner.

June 11

We went to a Captain's cocktail party and met some people whose names I can't remember.

June 15

Learned how to play Dominoes. Saw movie The Day They Robbed the Bank of England*—which stunk.*

June 16

Stopped at Algeciras and mailed all my letters. It is beautiful, surrounded by mountains and very warm. The buildings are white and clean. But I hear it's a filthy place.

June 17

Saw porpoises, 3 whales and the island of Majorca. Champagne in the veranda grill and dancing. Didn't dance at all because no one asked us except my German friend who affixiates me. So went to bed.

SCHOOL

I went to a convent school and our teachers were all nuns who wore habits. The habits consisted of black robes and white frilly headdresses out of which their pale faces would gaze at us with disapproval. Their wire-rimmed spectacles were oddly frightening, I'm not sure why. Their job was to teach us how to be Young Ladies. Our uniforms, checked jumpers with white blouses and Peter Pan collars, were perfectly hideous, I told my mother. Also, we had to wear clunky brown oxford shoes with navy blue knee socks. Even the most beautiful among us looked unattractive in the uniforms, which miraculously erased us, as if we were one body of useless females marooned on an island of useless nuns. Our school was a former estate belonging to a famous industrialist. Situated on a sort of farm, there were cows in the pastures and chickens in the barns. The nuns lived in cloisters and we lived in little cottages sprinkled around the property. In my memory of that time, the sky was always gray, and the tree branches bare and tangled, a pen and ink drawing, and we girls, sad little scribbles beneath, marching to mass or class or to the Quonset Hut. Our rooms at night were cold and the covers thin. It is as if we were preparing for a life of sacrifice, which, as it turns out, we were. My mother said, be thankful you have anything to wear at all.

ME AND MARLENE

Once I met Marlene Dietrich. I'd been working as a receptionist for the radio studios of WOR in New York. I was 18. It was my job to greet the guests when they arrived and give them a magazine. I met Jules Feiffer this way, even though I had no idea who he was. Others, too, illustrious and unknown to me. The talk-show hosts included Arlene Francis, Ed and Pegeen Kelly, Bob and Ray, Dorothy Kilgallen and her husband Dick ("Breakfast with Dorothy and Dick") and someone called Long John Nebel who I never met but could visualize, perhaps wrongly, as an Ichabod Crane-type character with a tubular gray neck. These days WOR is the home of right-wing talk show hosts Rush Limbaugh and Sean Hannity, among others, which depresses me. Imagine Michael Savage and Orson Welles appearing in the same column of "notable guests" names. I was an innocent girl with my own mistaken, largely inflated sense of class-worth and the reception area had been ratty looking and dim, washed in a yellow-ish pallor, the chairs brown, metal and uncomfortable. It was the early 60s, like Marlene, who was born in 1901.

I viewed last night for the first time the famous Josef von Sternberg movie *The Scarlet Empress* in which Marlene appears as a kittenish ingénue turned hard-boiled femme fatale: Marlene in ringlets, Marlene marcelled, Marlene rushing across a screen cluttered with von Sternberg *mise en scène*—enormous Hollywood constructions meant to simulate Russian statuary, dozens of staircases bisected with looming shadows—wearing white trousers and a white soldier's jacket profuse with military decorations.

Later in an interview included on the DVD, von Sternberg admits that the actors for him were always only spots of color to be ordered around and (I thought) nowhere is this more obvious than in *The Scarlet Empress* where Marlene appears and disappears in the midst of this aggressive prop world which looks (perhaps deliberately) fake.

In the WOR ladies room: imagine old black-and-white tiles and stalls with painted cream-colored metal doors and a row of porcelain sinks with soap dispensers through which you could see the vilely colored pink liquid soap. I was reapplying lipstick, a color from my mother's drawer called Bravo, and leaning into my image in the full-length chrome-framed mirror and I saw her behind me—Marlene. She was wearing a beautifully tailored beige suit with a fur-trimmed collar and even in her very high heels I was taller than she was. She was trying to see herself in the same full-length mirror I was occupying and I quickly moved aside and apologized.

Don't be silly, she said in her famous, imperious voice, and she stepped center stage to the mirror and turned this way and that way, finally asking me to check the seams on her stockings and tell her if they were straight. I supposed they were, I told her. (How straight was straight? I found myself worrying.) Then she asked me a series of questions that I don't remember. Very polite inquiries as those you would ask someone eighteen. In reality, I had dreams of becoming an actress, but I was too shy to say. Then she swanned out of the ladies, her fur collar touching the ends of her mouse-colored hair.

If I'd been a different girl, I would have followed Marlene out of the radio studio and into the lobby of the building. I would have crouched behind the candy-and-magazine stand and watched to see if she walked down the street like an ordinary person. I would have stalked her down Broadway and across 42nd Street, practicing the opening gambit that would change my life.

The minute you or anybody else knows what you are you are not it, you are what you or anybody else knows you are and as everything in living is made up of finding out what you are it is extraordinarily difficult really not to know what you are and yet to be that thing.

Gertrude Stein

WAR

And that's the way it was, intoned CBS's Walter Cronkite with his big megaphonic voice, his square head bobbing and looming commandingly into our living rooms. Across the screen, night after night, the names of the dead, their ranks and serial numbers.

Cronkite, NBC's young and handsome Peter Jennings, Huntly/ Brinkley on Channel 13. And the names of the daily dead. November 17, 1968 was the bloodiest day of the war—155 killed.

In between there were ads for Brylcreem or Pepsodent. Hair and teeth. Remnants.

We all protested, feeling virtuous. When the soldiers came home, we expressed our contempt. We who were privileged and did not serve.

LBJ was uncouth and bombastic. His bird-like wife planted bluebonnets all over the Texas highways.

I was a mother. I marched and protested. I smoked pot and wore flowers in my hair. Barefoot, I carried my infant daughter into the fray, into the lost light of the world.

C'EST MOI

As a child, I'd been the victim of various unkindnesses, no doubt brought on by my own difficult personality, a kind of failure to fit in coupled with disdain for others, even though I had very little self-awareness. To me the world existed inside of books, in the caves of my own imagination, so beautifully fed by books, and eventually, having cultivated the long habit of mind which held those dramas and visions and ethical appeals, I fell naturally into a habit of daydreaming, of insinuating myself into the center of those daydreams, in some heroic light or other. Had I only read *Madame Bovary* I would have perhaps recoiled from my own vanity and superficiality, but I was too lazy for Flaubert. When I finally got around to reading MB, I was too old to benefit from the lesson of poor Emma, having already married the wrong man.

MOTHERHOOD

I brought to this venture a few recipes and a mild interest in children. Having four kids in five years was very tiring. Every day I took a long nap as chaos raged around me. My visiting cousin observed that my children ran around naked while I read French poetry. Having been raised by hired help, I had no idea how to wash a floor (not with Ajax) and the washing machine intimidated me. I read French poetry and took naps and, in due course, accumulated more recipes: ratatouille, brown rice, homemade granola, zucchini cake—all loathed by the children.

JACKPOT

As if someone had fed lucky coins into a slot machine, children tumbled out of me in a clatter. Some of them flew around my head like shiny demons with red horns and others sat quietly in trees like Calvino's Baron. They ran races, baked cakes, threw pencils at their teachers, sulked in their rooms, read books, drew pictures of monsters devouring a village and pictures of flowers growing pleasantly around a white house, or they simply scribbled on the walls with purple magic marker and laughed about it. They smeared my lipstick over their tiny chapped lips, stumbled around in my high heels, polished off the scalloped edges of an entire Thanksgiving pie, and, once, opened their Christmas presents the week before without apologizing. They fought each other like vicious animals eager for the taste of blood. Shrieking in the backseat of the car, squirming under the covers of my bed, riffling through my clothes with their sticky paws in order to make a tent, always singing, crying, imploring, eating, vomiting and swearing, I was never not-alone. They crawled into my ears and infected my dreams. They joined hands and formed a ring-around-the-rosy circle, trapping me in the middle—a monkey—spinning, trying to get my bearings. They stole my heart, by dint of some magic. And then suddenly, they vanished, and the air was calm and sweet and the trees were unfettered and everything was so, so quiet, I thought I would die.

A MEMOIR

My first husband was very handsome. His blond hair had a habit of falling charmingly over one eye. His nose was very straight like the nose of a saint. He wore Brooks Brothers suits which, when he left us to live in the woods, he would drape over tree branches.There he made little fires and cooked food wrapped in tin foil, which impressed the children.

The truth is I made him leave. He was a stockbroker but that isn't why. On the way home from New Jersey in a snowstorm he drove like a maniac. Crossing the George Washington Bridge, I begged him to slow down or stop so I could drive. So he pulled over and got out of the car. The children were sleeping in the back seat. I climbed into the driver's seat and followed him as he staggered along the side of the George Washington Bridge, bombarded by pellets of snow. After a while, he got in the car and called me a cunt.

For years I hung on, though it was like hanging onto a ledge of a burning building. Beneath me, gulls cracked through clouds.

GRATITUDE

In the 70s, I had a series of sad but spectacular cars. I had a red 65 Mustang convertible with a hole in the gas tank, A Rover TC2000 that wouldn't go in reverse ("a metaphor for my life," I used to quip), an old round Studebaker with no back seat and several VWs, blighted in various ways, and eventually inoperable. In between broken vehicles, I would hitchhike, often with my youngest, the infant Rachel, in my arms. We would hitchhike all over, even on the New England Thruway. It's a wonder we weren't murdered.

One wintry day we were picked up by a tiny old woman in a long, yellow 1969 Oldsmobile Cutlass Supreme. She pulled over to the side of the road and we scrambled into the back. She drove as if she were maneuvering a boat on a roiling ocean. The car rocked back and forth (bad shocks?) and from my vantage in the back, I could see her beige scalp through her beige hair and her fierce little hands on the wheel. When she dropped us off at the exit, I told her she shouldn't pick up hitchhikers, that it could be dangerous. I really said this, though I was grateful for the ride.

THE SECRET

When my kids were little, I visited a psychic. She was a heavyset woman who wore a colorful muumuu. She greeted me warmly and told me she'd be just a sec. I waited in her living room, which was littered with cat toys, though there was no cat in sight.

I wondered how people could live comfortably amidst so much clutter. There seemed to be too much furniture—one too many couches and chairs and wall hangings and small tables covered with an abundance of ceramic figurines and no place for the eye to rest. If a window had been available, I would have rested my eyes there, on a tree or a hill, something that seemed to be in its rightful place. But there were dizzying checkered drapes on the windows and these were closed.

Even the bathroom, which I visited while waiting, was filled with unnecessary accoutrements. Toilet tissue covers made of fleece and little crocheted sayings on wall plaques and several large and noisy clocks. On a small table next to the loo sat a book of jokes as well as a Bible. The bathtub was painted blue and above it, on a spool, a neon plastic fish twirled rapidly, as if driven by a motor.

Here you are! said the psychic when I emerged from the bathroom. She was drying her hands on a dishtowel. Sorry, but I had to finish up with the dishes and I had to pop these brownies out of the oven, she said. She took my hand in her moist, warm ones. You seem like a nice person, she said. She studied my palm intently. Yes, she said. A nice person with many children. Yes, I agreed. I wanted to ask what would happen to us and what I should do in life. I was uncertain about things and proceeded through each day wearing my uncertainty like a sweater. That is why I came to the psychic in the first place. I waited patiently for her counsel, but instead she offered me a brownie. It was an incredibly delicious brownie and I was not ungrateful. The secret is sour cream, she told me. Take some home for the children.

LARKS

I always thought Larks was a stupid name for a cigarette. They came in a maroon package and boasted innovative charcoal filters that tasted like cheap men's cologne. I never liked them, but I smoked them out of loyalty to my husband who worked for the manufacturer. Thus, Larks were a constant in my life then, cartons strewn around our dwelling much like, in a later age, my shoes would be. Cartons opened and unopened, cigarette packages on every surface of our lives along with the burnt and smoldering butts and the ubiquitous green haze in the air of the world.

We were always smoking, in other words. It was as if breathing were impossible without the rancid taste of the Lark. In those days, we lived in Puerto Rico and I'd just given birth. I vowed our tiny baby would be ready for anything. I hefted her into the flimsy infant seat of that era and jiggled her on my lap as the prop plane hurtled us to St. Thomas. Cigarette in hand, I breast fed her everywhere, in the glamorous courtyards of five-star hotels and in the grimy corners of discos. Even in that prop plane, careening in our seats, I brushed the ash from her infant head and we both tugged greedily.

PANIC

Once my father made me drive his Oldsmobile over a small bridge because he was afraid to. If I hadn't been there, he would have made himself do it.

I avoid highways, freeways, main roads with traffic and any megalith of road with speeding cars and vast expanses, where one is supposed to drive and drive into some nightmarish infinity far from home.

It was a small country bridge flanked by leafless trees (winter in the northeast) and little patches of dirty snow. I drove fast, wanting to get home, away from my father's fear.

I am prone to panic attacks when I am alone behind the wheel of a car. When someone else is driving I forget all about my panic. A panic attack is born of intense fear. Your own body is harboring the ticking IED. There is an imperative to run, but where to? You are the enemy.

My father spoke very little about phobias though I believe he, too, was prone. He didn't like to ride 43 floors up in an elevator to a restaurant, for example.

Common knowledge: If you speak about a panic attack you might bring one on.

My father had been telling me stories about his trials with my mother. These stories made my skin crawl.

There was a time when I loved driving, being alone in the car made me feel free to let my mind wander instead of being compelled to take action. This was before cell phones, when I was married. I listened to the radio, but we lived in the country and the reception wasn't great. I drove the babysitter home at night and daydreamed. When I got home, I stayed a while in the driveway in front of the big pine tree so I could finish being alone in the car.

My father did not have a normal man's life with my mother, did I know what he meant?

He meant: My mother had polio and would no longer fuck him.

Listening to my father's confidences made me feel as if someone were holding my head under water.

Sometimes when I am driving, I make myself become hyperconscious in the moment of driving and this is all it takes to get the panic swimming up.

Every day I have to drive somewhere, and I've made sure my old car is comfortable. Like a well-appointed living room, it has heated seats, a good sound system, a magnetized vase of fresh flowers jittering on the dash, various charger plugs for various devices, a padded steering wheel cover, two cup holders in case I want to alternate between vodka and coffee, a nice slip-out slot for spare change, side pockets for papers, many ashtrays, a sunroof for ventilation and so on. People honk at me when I go too slow, enjoying myself and my cigarette, back when I smoked cigarettes.

My father died before Google, before iPhones, before cup holders. He was afraid of heights but not anything else. He was a man's man and once told my mother not to purchase any books written by women.

I had an idea I would write an essay about a very particular thing today, but I forget what it was. I remember thinking about it while in the car, then it vanished from the screen.

The 21st-century trope for memory: a screen covered with information, just as quickly deleted. Driving and forgetting, I may have been on the verge of apprehension because to return from my destination involved going up an unfamiliar road and making a U-turn around the road divider. I hadn't counted on the road divider and to distract myself I thought of an idea for an essay. It was a big topic, something I cared about, but not politics. I had been reading a book about resuscitation after death. I had been reading a book about boredom. I had been thinking about the new restaurant that opened in our neighborhood. Perhaps it was about memory.

It's only just occurred to me that I wrecked that husband's life. In those days, I drove a Volvo with bad brakes. One had to coast to a stop.

My father gave me a car for my graduation from high school, but then he took it back. There is a photo of me standing beside it—a white Chevrolet Catalina convertible—looking uneasy, as if I knew its future.

I was stopped by a cop when I was a teenager, but I flirted with him and he let me off. In those days, I was fearless.

A bird is not a car, but that flight has some of the magnificence of the solo drive, for the bird. Imagine powering oneself across state lines, from cold to warm air, state line to state line, greener each day. It would be like the dream of flying I love to have.

3,000 pounds of steel is not a natural shell for the human animal. Why should we go anywhere?

I know people who've lived in tee pees, perfectly happy. I suppose they become familiar with the birds. Today a mockingbird imitated my ring tone.

In any case, my father would not admit to being frightened of anything. He lived in the era when men were—

Pre-ringtone.

Some birds make long migrations along flyways. You can Google pictures of them walking on shorelines, on their way to the future in joyful expanses of air.

Still, as indicated, I am happiest when someone else is in charge, even a machine is better than me being in charge. I hope I am alive when people travel in cars that drive themselves.

I cannot imagine my father as a bird (heights). If reincarnated, he would be a lion or a wolf, some animal of prey, some lusting voracious thing. If I could I would follow a bird.

This may be a good time to mention that once, in a day-dreamy inadvertency, I followed a stranger to their driveway.

Certain birds, the shrike, for example, scream. Cockatiels,

parrots. The shrike makes a bee line for earth while screaming: a kid on a roller coaster.

Kurt Cobain said, "birds scream at the top of their lungs every day to warn us of the horrible truth." Two things: I am not a fan of Kurt Cobain, and birds, like God, are unlikely to issue warnings.

When my father screamed: a brusque impatient sound, full of suffering grievance. I was not my father's fan either.

Today I drove three places. The streets were calm. No IEDs in sight.

As if my body could improvise an explosive device.

That Volvo was the scariest car I ever drove. Brakeless, I had to maneuver very skillfully at lights—you can imagine. The husband whose life I ruined: well, I just got fed up.

That husband: Handsome but flawed.

As I have seen a swan with bootless labour swim against the tide, and spend her strength with over-matching waves. As usual, Shakespeare offers a good metaphor for a marriage, I think, as well as driving when something at the core of one's being doesn't want to drive. My bootless cries! My bootless feet!

Overcast still and I drive in a murk of light. I drive fast these days, slip into the left lane in front of a black Toyota, speed through the light in the nick of time.

I love the way they look, a flock of them cutting across the sky, a scattering of dark eyebrows, soaring. Or envelopes containing messages. Over-matching waves. Under which I am held, trying to scream. I left the husband in the nick of time.

In my former life, my father said, sadly, let me tell you about your mother. He gripped the wheel fiercely. On the verge, he pulled over and asked me to drive.

GURUS

For a while I was devoted to a guru and, as such, was referred to as a devotee. This yearning to know the future. I could have become a drug addict, but I chose the guru. I sat on a cushion in a vast hall that once hosted Borscht Belt comedians. I tried not to think about it. *My wife made me a chocolate mousse but the antlers got stuck in my throat. Doctor, I hear a ringing in my ears. Don't answer it.* The good old days. There were remnants—a flocked velvet curtain flanking the stage on which my guru sat silently on his throne. A cigarette burn in the parquet floor near my cushion. Mirrors everywhere, gold-framed and glitzy. There had once been laughter and smoke. There had once been cocktails in glasses shaped like tulips, tiny umbrellas twirling inside them, drunken tuxedo-wearing men, ties askew, stumbling around. A woman in a green gown, hair in a sleek chignon, could have been me. She sat like a manikin, face frozen and unamused, her spidery eyelashes weighing her eyelids like cages. She smoked a cigarette with a white filter and, after a while, she draped a scrap of mink around her shoulders.

TYPEWRITER

I wanted to be a painter. Hadn't I gotten an honorable mention in our town's Halloween window painting contest? Hadn't my still life—apple, skull, violin—been featured in our movie theater preteen show? Hadn't I majored in Art at my college even though the professor told me women could never be great artists? Nevertheless, when my kids scribbled all over my paintings in purple magic marker, permanently altering the mood of the pastel-colored fantasies of flying horses and ballerinas, I decided to pack it in. I hauled out my grandfather's old Underwood typewriter—another beautiful object to vanish from my life, along with a set of Waterford crystal, a moiré-covered dressmakers' manikin and a 1960 Studebaker in celadon.

GOATS

Retreads is what they used to call older women—more precisely, older but not so old as to be of no use at all. Tired we were, worn out, craftily patched up, barely serviceable, only a snippet of service left before we imploded. I recollect this from among a wealth of derogatives from that other era, when men were men more absolutely, more stridently than now, and women had a shelf life.

I recall myself at an age not so long ago, my hair long and tangled, my youth having recently flown, the wake of it jittering behind me, a rose leached of color. Allow me to reinterpret. I was a rose leached of color, craftily patched up, past my sell-by date. But not quite old, as it happens.

A man called me up and asked if he could take me for a picnic. Fine, I said. I always said fine. There was something slimy and entitled about him. I should have known better. He brought along a guitar which he played abstractedly for a while—and this part sounds like a fairy tale—a little troop of wild goats circled us. We were way out somewhere in Mexico, in a field near a hot spring. It was a nice day. The goats were small and white and delicate.

Like a fairy tale, it should have been charming. As it was, I allowed the man to fuck me. He was so insistent. I was a little afraid, but not terrified.

Later I repeated this story to a woman I would also allow to fuck me. Nothing about her scared me, but in those days I felt I had to acquiesce. I was a retread, they said at the time. Such expressions made me feel small, unsettled and repulsive. I was lucky for any attention at all.

POET

For ten years or so I was unemployed. I'd been a single mother in grad school and spent at least half of that time on Public Assistance. My caseworker was a tiny woman with curled hair and rosy cheeks, like an impeccably groomed doll. She sat in a big chair, wielding the enormous directory that contained the names of all possible jobs and their codes. I'd told her I was a poet. Her face knotted with anxiety as she flipped the slippery pages, carefully examining words with a magnifying glass. She cleared her throat a few times as she read. When at last she slammed the book shut, she looked truly regretful. I'm so sorry, she announced, but it is impossible at this juncture to find you any employment. As if it were her personal failure and not the fault of my stupid profession.

THE FUNNY HAT STORY

In an effort to get off Public Assistance, I worked at the corporate headquarters of a big chemical company. I was an admin assistant and was lucky to get the job since typing and alphabetizing were not my strong points. But I'd done a stint as a proofreader and my duties were to proof audits full of numbers. I used to say that my boss, Mr. V, was himself like a numeral, so dry and colorless was he. Daily, he hung over my shoulder, his cheek fluttering against mine, bathing me in bad breath. The best part of that job was a big lunchroom with free food. There I quickly struck up a friendship with a girl called Georgina, who was very beautiful, too beautiful to be a secretary. She told me she often went on trips with her bosses and other bosses and was paid well for her company. I had a thrilling glimmer of what that meant, and I asked a lot of questions. Soon I received a phone call from a man who invited me to do the same. I remembered this person, a friend of Georgina's, very handsome with a cold authority I found dangerous and attractive. He drove around the big wigs in a limousine. "You have something I want and I have something you want, do you know what I mean?" he said. A week after I turned him down, I was fired. I was told it was because I wore funny hats to work.

THE MOVIE STAR

On a cinematic screen people look larger than life, gods from another dimension. Thus, we come to believe they are giants, unapproachable and dangerous. In person, we have trouble recognizing them. Such was my first encounter with Paul Newman, whose children attended the school where I taught science.

I was not qualified to teach science and the fact that I was able to land this job is still a mystery to me. I had taken one general science class in high school—my girls' convent school, where it was thought that women would never become scientists anyway, so why bother—and a brief biology class taught by a nun who wore big round glasses and was easily intimidated. The reproductive pages were cut out of our biology text books, pages we imagined contained the best dirty secrets of grownups, and, indeed, would have been relevant to us girls whose pre-ordained, life's work was to be the production and care of babies.

Despite all this, years later and having dutifully created my own babies, I was hired by a dark-haired man called Martin whom

I later slept with. Eventually I taught a unit on sex ed since I was having a lot of sex at the time, which I supposed made me an expert. In any case, I knew more than Bob, my co-worker in science, who never lost an opportunity to announce he had graduated from Princeton. Bob did know a lot. He had studied science in college—perhaps he had been a physics major. One thing he didn't know was sex. His feeble attempt to teach sex ed was met with jeers and giggles from the students. He said, for example, that it took 20 to 25 minutes for a man to acquire an erection. Even sixth graders knew this was wrong. This is where I stepped in with my superior knowledge based on experience. It was the 70s; we were all sluts except Bob.

Other than that, I took the kids on nature walks—the school bordered a wood and a gorge—and collected their dreams for my expert interpretation. Such were my ideas about science. The challenge of that job was how to avoid the actual teaching of science *qua* science, sticking instead to topics I excelled at.

I first met Paul Newman when he knocked on my classroom door; I was in the middle of teaching a unit on the manipulation of crowds, which I'd vaguely intended to be a class on advertising. We were creating an absurd questionnaire to take to grocery stores and see how many people we could hustle into dutifully completing a survey that didn't make sense. In retrospect, it had been a kind of performance piece. A line of questions went:

Do you believe in preservatives?

How many?

Have there been related problems?

Which relations? (circle one, mother, father, cousin, daughter, sister).

Most people were courteous and calm; they filled out the thing with the pencil we provided, carefully circling choices that were not choices—(*what level of education have you completed? circle one: 1, 2, 3*). Others were irate, loudly protesting that the survey was *illogical.*

The movie star knocked. He wore blue jeans and a denim shirt—his uniform—his excellent salt and pepper hair was neatly combed. He was very short, shorter than me. On account of his stature and his workmanlike clothes, I mistook him for the guy we hired to fix the air conditioning unit in my classroom. Wait outside, I ordered. And the surprising thing is that he obeyed me.

COMPULSION

The *amazona vittata* or the Puerto Rican Parrot reside in El Yunque forest, a rainforest in the Caribbean National Park. Typically 11 inches in length and weighing about eight ounces, the parrot is only a bit larger than a parakeet. In coloring it is that livid green typical of all parrots, wild and domestic. They have black dots of eyes surrounded by a ring of white that to me look like a child's first drawing of eyes, simultaneously startled and insane, with a dapper red fringe above a voluptuous bill. Their feathers are so soft that in photographs they look like fur. When Columbus landed in Puerto Rico in the 15th century, he was greeted by millions of these birds, but by 1965, which is when this story takes place, there were only about 60 left in the wild.

When we lived in Puerto Rico, my first husband and myself, we were invited to observe the Puerto Rican Parrot with Nathan Leopold, a man newly sprung from a life sentence for the murder of a fourteen-year-old Bobby Franks, a legendary "perfect" crime. Leopold served 33 years before he was released for good behavior, whereupon he exiled himself to Puerto Rico where he devoted himself to ornithology. In 1958 he'd published a book called *Checklist of Birds of Puerto Rico and the Virgin Islands.*

It was a thrill for my handsome husband to be invited to gawk not especially at the birds but at the murderer. I wanted nothing to do with neither the man nor the parrot and stayed at home in my cement shack, gazing at the piles of laundry I didn't feel like washing and reading *Madame Bovary*. Later, with a mixture of fear and pride, my husband reported that Leopold had made a pass at him.

In retrospect, I regret not having taken the opportunity to meet the famous murderer/ornithologist, to have filed away a whiff of his brilliance and madness and demeanor. I do not regret that first reading of *Madame Bovary*, however, which for me had not been a cautionary tale, but a tale of liberation, never mind the consequences.

TV OR NO TV

For years, on principle, I did not own a TV. My children drew pictures and acted out stories and were annoyingly loud, but untainted. Then my father, to spite me, bought us a television. The children were thrilled. A small, weirdly heavy portable, it was plunked by my father on a table in our living room blocking our view of trees and a lake. On Saturday mornings, the kids could be found glued to the screen, watching cartoons. From the kitchen I caught sound bites of Wilma and Fred enacting the vicissitudes of modern American life, Wilma the cautionary voice behind her buffoon of a husband—the buffoon who nonetheless was the breadwinner, the outside-the-box-thinker, the adventurer. Television was teaching my children what was what in the world. I should be grateful. Otherwise these same mesmerized children would be racing around knocking things over and screaming and hitting one another and sticking their grubby fingers in the pancake batter I was mixing up, like Wilma. Luckily, there was no shouting Fred in the vicinity of my life.

HORTENSIA

Hortensia was a Mexican fortune teller with long red hair and yellow-flecked hazel eyes ringed with charcoal liner. She was done up for tourist trade in a gypsy dress and lots of jewelry, silver hooped earrings, many strands of beads around her neck and metal bracelets up to her elbows. Her arms jangled and chimed when she moved them, the only sound in the shadowy room. I rested my hands on a small table and, when instructed, I cut the tarot deck into three piles. I was, as usual, lost in my life and wanting direction. I'd lived in Mexico for a time and though my Spanish was not good, I managed to meet people here and there, to form quick intimate friendships, and then to see them dissipate, as if I'd hallucinated them. Sometimes, when walking the beautiful cobbled streets, I'd think this is the happiest I've ever been. Other times I'd be wracked with emotional pain, an intruder in a world that was otherwise perfect. Hortensia turned over a card and predicted that I would fall in love. She turned over the next card and said this love would not last. She was about to turn over a third card when she was seized with a coughing fit and had to leave the room. I sat there for a while, enjoying the darkness and gazing at the candle she had lit, its melting wax forming nice, fat drips onto the small dish beneath it. Who doesn't love melting candle wax? I fashioned a bird sitting on a tree hovering over a village of sleepy houses. A man emerged from one of these houses wearing pajamas. He walked down a pathway, fetched his newspaper and shaking it open he sighed so loudly it sent a shiver down my spine. A kid rode a bike down the street. A woman hung clothes on a clothesline. It was peaceful there. It had that Grecian-urn quality of *unravish'dment* until I destroyed it and Hortensia delivered the bad news of the rest of my life.

ALICE'S RESTAURANT, REDUX

1

I'd been living in Purdys, a train-stop village in Northern Westchester county, consisting of a market owned by a Mrs. Plevka, whose cats used to squat hairily over the pastries. Besides the children, I was growing and tending a magnificent marijuana plant, almost five feet high with dark, glossy, unmistakable leaves, which I'd stupidly situated in the entryway.

The time two policemen made their way up the front walk, I instructed the children to stand in front of the plant, stretch out their arms, and not move a muscle. For once, they obeyed me. The police, as it turns out, were there not because of illegal drugs but because when I last moved, a few boxes of my garbage were discovered in a Good Will drop off and I was being cited for littering. I snatched the subpoena from the short cop, blocking as well as I could the children and the plant itself whose distinctive leaves fanned out from behind their heads anyway. A more perceptive police duo would have spotted it in a heartbeat.

2

Eventually, I was tried for this littering infraction, but by then I was already in another village in another house, one that overlooked a lake, and had dumped the pot plant. I've told this story many times because it is one of those stories you tell once you have escaped a particular past. The Purdys flat, what I can remember of it, was narrow and dark and depressed us all. I was on Public Assistance and my choices were limited, but I had an aesthetic sense that kept us on the move.

I arrived at the courthouse—more like someone's garage—and there the witnesses to my offense had gathered: the short policeman; a balding retiree with a stammer, apparently a police *volunteer*, who had cleverly tracked me to my address by way of the mail in the trash I was accused to have dumped; and a man with a faintly Scandinavian accent wearing a yellow nylon windbreaker who, in evidence of my bad character, presented to the court several overdue and/or shut-off notices from utility companies, also culled from my trash. I explained to the judge that it was an honest mistake—trash in goodwill, good will in trash, single mother, blah blah—but the serious Scandinavian, I could see, was unmoved by my defense and stood by hopefully, waiting for my conviction.

3

After the judge let me go, he asked me out on a date, because that's the way it was in the 70s. He was a large, awkward man with a big head of black hair, not at all terrible looking. But he lived with his mom, which struck me as a bad sign, so I turned him down.

ROSA

Rosa was my CETA co-worker at the Women's Commission. She had long, soft, dark hair pulled back to show her nice, multiply-pierced earlobes. She was kind and calm, a combination of traits I have longed for my entire life.

Our boss, an energetic woman devoted to the cause of women nationally and internationally (as she put it), insisted we work around the clock. We were single mothers with children, but that did not faze our dedicated boss who hailed from Munich and who, to demonstrate her superior female energy, performed a complicated set of calisthenics each day in the park near her house and walked her beige dog. In her capacious office, appointed with a nice sofa and a picture of her homeland—a silver lake and a row of blue snow-capped mountains—she availed herself of a daily nap, her beige dog snoozing beside her.

Rosa and I missed school conferences, baseball games, confirmation ceremonies, Christmas plays and recitals. We wrote letters, processed discrimination complaints, organized group mailings, made posters, and called our local and state representatives. We found housing for the homeless, applied for food stamps for the starving, we soothed and cajoled the troubled. Around 7, after we had devoted the last shred of our energy to the national and international causes of women, we staggered home to our families, having earned, roughly, three bucks an hour.

NO PICKLES

I met my second husband at No Pickles. I was feeding my children at the counter and he came in for a snack. No Pickles was owned and managed by Barbara and me—it was situated in a pavilion on Peach Lake, where we lived. We paid no rent, promising instead to supply the diabetic residents with healthy dinners. We made hamburgers and hot dogs, served a variety of ice creams and pies and, once in a while, an excellent chicken dish crafted by Barbara, who was a chef—but no pickles. Sad to say, the diabetics went by the wayside. After a while we ran out of food, mainly because we were serving our children and not making any money. I usually hung out on the porch writing poems while people helped themselves from the cash register. Once some friends dropped by and introduced me to a man whose eyes were the same color as mine. He was appalled at my management style. I gave him the remaining scoop of vanilla ice cream and a Chunky on the house, thereby launching the next phase of my life.

MAD MEN

We all loved that TV series *Mad Men* for its gorgeous, neurotic characters and its soap-opera melodramas, but most of all for its "look." Creator Matthew Wiener insisted that every aspect of the *mis-en-scène*—the magazines on the tables, the brands of booze, the cars, the kitchen décor, the fedoras, the ties, the women's midi skirts, even the TV shows—conformed to life in the 1960s. As it happened, I was alive in the 60s. A freshly minted college grad with a degree in studio art, I'd landed a job at an ad agency in NYC on Madison Avenue. I think my father must have arranged my job with BBD&O, as I cannot imagine anyone hiring a person with such a mediocre crop of artwork—watercolor illustrations for poems I'd written, a few tempera drawings suggestive of Bemelmans. I had not gone to art school, but to a small liberal arts girls' college (as they were called then—it would be years before such places were called women's colleges). I lived in Greenwich Village with my friend Kathleen who was more adventurous than I was—I have a memory of her spending the night at some guy's apartment in the days when we didn't do that.

Even though I was given the glorious title of Assistant Art Director, my job was to stand in the paste-up room laboring over large pots of rubber cement which made me high before I knew what it meant to be stoned. I was the only girl in the art department—if there was a secretary she was off somewhere and invisible, and writing this now I wonder if secretaries were always invisible in those days, cramped into corners, hunched behind desks, heads down, hard at work over their typewriters. I was lucky not to be a secretary for this reason and also because I would have been a terrible secretary. I had taken a secretarial test and it turned out that not only were my typing skills below par, but I was hopeless at alphabetizing.

I worked with the guys doing a job that was one step up from janitor despite the fancy title. I smeared rubber cement on the backs of cut out images and pasted them on other pieces of paper or I worked with a hot press machine, which looked like a giant panini press, and whose purpose was also to affix paper to paper. The best thing about the job was the kind of sweatshop camaraderie and the fact that no one expected me to dress up. I had been offered employment at *Vogue* Magazine (also via a connection) and had turned it down when I saw the parade of glamorous women in designer suits swan in and out of the editorial offices. I was perceptive enough to know I could never keep up.

Of all the characters on that show I related most to Peggy, of course, the girl in a man's world, bullied and flirted with alternatively, though unlike Peggy I had no particular ambition. The ad business struck me, even then, as shallow and manipulative and I couldn't see myself as climbing any kind of ladder, much less that one. Also, I was about to be married. My engagement picture appeared in the NYT, looking unrecognizably aristocratic and the guys had a good time teasing me about it. For a going away present they gave me a rag mop that they dyed brown, in honor of my usual hairdo, and they all autographed the pole. On my last day, one of the art directors whispered me a word of advice, which was to pull myself together for marriage, by which I think he meant wear nicer clothes and comb my hair.

Recently I met a person who had done some scholarly work on *Mad Men* (because in this era we do that kind of thing) and she asked me if Weiner's representation was accurate. I had to think about it because something had been off in that show. Then it occurred to me—it was the dirt. There was no dirt in MM, but it had been a filthy world back in the 60s in NYC.

Trash littered the streets, the offices were dim, the walls and floors grimy and everyone smoked. We wouldn't think twice about throwing a candy wrapper or even a sandwich wrapper into the streets or even on the floor along with the cigarettes we stomped out. My new friend pointed out to me that there was one scene in *Mad Men* where Don and Betty are picnicking with the kids and they rather pointedly throw their trash into an otherwise pristine field. But this was the only nod to the filth of those times and that TV trash was an immaculate construction of the prop department.

There were no Bridget Rileys on the walls, much less the occasional Rothko or Hoffman clone. It was as if Matthew Weiner imported into the dregs of the 60s our 21st-century sensibility—this spotless new world we live in without the litter of cigarette butts, among our updated iPhones and computers and shiny streets equipped, as if for a TV series, with silent, well-behaved pedestrians.

In fact, it is as if we are always on display in our reconstituted mid-century homes with our freshly balayaged hair and our designer jeans, arranged on sectionals we ordered from Design Within Reach, squirting our perfect coffees from Nespresso's, driving our silent, ubiquitous Priuses through the calm avenues of our villages. Even I have managed to make myself presentable over the years, as if Big Brother were filming me glide through my life. No wonder everyone is shooting everyone else!

My friend the *Mad Men* expert sipped her coffee. You think?

It was a beautiful morning and we'd been sitting on my backyard porch, a pastiche of a place, with mismatched chairs, a wicker loveseat with chipped paint, a colorfully fringed Thai parasol, a Buddha with a smashed nose, three silver globes hanging from a rafter, an arrangement of papier-mâché candle sticks on a shelf next to a glass head and strings of tea-lights hammered into the concrete walls. A few feet away in the giant presiding mesquite, chimed the soulful notes of the mourning doves. A fat green lizard slid out of the sun and disappeared beneath a chair. A hummingbird helicoptered by, its wings as speedy as bullets. Time stood still.

SORROW

I fly back into those lost years and they cannot contain me. I am mid-flight, inventing a fairy tale, while around me the world falls apart. The table is set so carefully, forks on the left side, knives and spoons on the right, while not so far away someone is in handcuffs and someone else is weeping uncontrollably. Someone wearing a black hood is kneeling down. One hopes God exists.

Rachel, my beloved youngest, climbs on a motorcycle, smashes her good brain and ruins her life. She lives in a room with a new roommate. Carmella, whom we love, has been moved. Now there is an ill-tempered person who lies in a narrow bed and watches a small, noisy TV, day and night. The "inmates" are a good 75 years older than I am, Rachel says, to be funny. Her friend Alma has Alzheimer's, I think, and Marie, a holocaust survivor, is nearly 100. I proceed to Rachel like a horse with blinders, not wanting to catch an eye, not wanting to engage. Are you Rachel's mother? Where are you going? Where will you take Rachel? But I cannot ignore Stuart, who is young, sandy-haired, hollow-eyed, with his head resting on his own shoulder. Does he really watch that TV? Is he listening? Is he your friend? I ask Rachel. No, she says.

I *is only a convenient term for somebody who has no real being. Lies will flow from my lips but there may be perhaps some truth mixed up with them; it is for you to seek out this truth and to decide whether any part of it is worth keeping.*

Virginia Woolf

TELEVISION

From a neighbor's house, the happy strains of a party and once again we are outsiders. There is laughter, music, the lilt of easy conversation between adults of goodwill, people who actually like each other. Our own life, by comparison, is lackluster, dull, often complicated and frustrating. Our relationships are fraught with difficulties, too often lacking in ease and warmth. We are lonely, plagued with loneliness, suffocated by solitude. No wonder our presence is not required at such a gathering. But were we to peek through the picture window of the party house, we would find no lively human guests, but a flat screen teeming with beautiful, animated simulacra and a person asleep on a couch.

BINGE

Have you never binged on a TV series and in the middle of *Big Little Lies*, hit pause, got out the Häagen-Dazs and spoon, skipped the dish, then back to crushing on Shailene Woodley, or three series of *Mad Men*, all night long and into Sunday, Elizabeth Moss aka Peggy evolving into a power bitch, with a package of Oreo double creams or box of saltines with melted Velveeta or fried onions in range-fed butter puddled on the creamy surface of tomato red pepper soup with a crank of Himalayan salt, alongside *Ozark*'s Jason Bateman so wide-eyed innocent for that role which is why he's perfect and Laura Linney so fucking sinister alongside a block of cheddar that you keep scraping with the cheese planer into the thinnest, orange-ist slices that you roll around a pickle or dip into a tub of mayo while *Orange is the New Black* at the edge of your seat (is it rage?) so you gotta keep at the pistachios, already shelled and salted, and a tube of chocolate Neccos, miraculously recovered in an old suitcase, thank you, dissolve on your tongue during the great array of BBC shows like *Broadchurch, Happy Valley, Last Tango in Halifax* or the Australian *Offspring* and *Sisters*, while shoving handfuls of popcorn and home-made fudge into the aching pie-hole, when finally *The Marvelous Mrs. Maisel* (season 2) infuses you with such unlikely hope and optimism that you eat an entire cake, icing first, and a bag of Fritos....??

TOUCH

My father believed—or, to be fair, it seemed to me my father believed—that my worth was wrapped up in having children and, after that, I was more or less useless, better off out of everyone's hair. Perhaps all men of his generation believed that about women. Divorced women were especially baffling; what were they for?

I had not intended to write about my father, but here he crops up. When he died, I was by his side in the hospital. His hair was a bright beautiful silver and I smoothed it back from his forehead, something I had not dared to do when he was alive. I watched the breath leave his body, the monitors go mute. His hair, so soft, did not change at the moment of his death. Still silver, soft, under my hand for the first and last time.

FULL DISCLOSURE

My son is in jail right now. He has been languishing—this is not the right word—there for months. I've lost count. Drugs, of course it's always drugs.

When he calls (collect) he sounds more or less fine, more or less contented or at least on an even keel. They are giving him lithium for his bipolar disorder. He spent a long time in solitary lockdown and during that time I did not hear from him. What did he do exactly? I'll tell you later.

My brother has a condo in Florida and other houses in other places. When he calls, he is cleaning dust from a closet. He is choking on dust, he reports. He had a cleaning service, but they did not get to the closet. Now the plumber and TV cable guy are there. He cannot talk, really, even though he called to complain about the dust. Also, because I am asking him about money and he has no answers for me. Don't ask me all these questions, he says. Talk to a lawyer.

TWO VERSIONS

It wasn't until I approached my twilight years that I became more certain of my mission in life. My daughter suffers. My son suffers. I am the mother of those who suffer, whose hands are tied against the pain of others, who is doomed to witness the agony of those I love. Thus, I see myself, also suffering, also helpless, and doomed—though my suffering is not as much as theirs, a fact which increases my suffering. Likewise, each day brings a little ray of hope. That is also who I am. She who wears different hats, and designer sunglasses, she who listens to Blossom Dearie, who cooks a complicated *boeuf en daube* and takes photographs of miniature cities arranged on the kitchen counter.

THAT HUSBAND

The husband who years ago met Nathan Leopold and drank too much and frequently hit me is now living in a school bus in the Arizona desert. He has a collection of stray dogs and lives in such impressive squalor that the clean-up guy we hired had to wear a hazmat suit.

That husband doesn't care if he lives in squalor or not. He doesn't care that he lives alone and hardly sees anyone. He has guns, he listens to right-wing radio, his favorite author is Jack London. He likes living in the desert, keeping an eye out for "illegals." With his guns at the ready. A stray dog stole onto his bed in the middle of the night and gave birth to a litter of puppies right by his head. It is hard to believe any of this. He calls his children twice a year—his birthday and Father's Day.

I went to see him in the hospital after his stroke. They had shaved his beard and cut his hair; his eyes were a pale, lost blue, and familiar to me after all these years. He inquired repeatedly after his dogs.

WHAT IF

We all know that show *Hoarders*, where a television crew goes into someone's house at the request of a relative and cleans up after those who can't seem to throw anything away. In one episode a woman, not able to make it to her front door over the piles of shopping bags and plastic bottle collections, had to be hauled from a window. In another, the owner was ultimately placed in a facility. It is a sad show that marks not only the depths of neurosis a person can sink to, but our fascination with such depths. It is as if watching these shows provides immunity to those specific horrors. Trapped on the flat screen, a preposterous reality unfolds, one that can never include us. If there's anything we've learned, it's the difference between our lives and those sleek, fantastical, televisual representations. That mess is not our mess, right?

NOSTOS

Between Rachel's Home and this home, there are two and a half miles. My home with its art on the walls, the French doors through which whose slatted wooden blinds my Tibetan flags drift beneath the big mesquite branch, my patio chairs, my little ornamental pig with the pleasingly green legs purchased at the gem show a few years ago—

and her Home with its soulless gigantic space for eating and watching TV and listening to the volunteer entertainers, its yellow vinyl floors, its stained reception sofa, its instructive signs, its white boards with the trivia of the day, and the little room she shares with two others, her space about a quarter of my own bedroom and separated by a maroon curtain, her meals served from a big smelly meal cart, pre-plated, the string beans a dull green, the mashed potatoes out of a box.

Home, suggests James Wood in a lecture I listened to on YouTube recently, and he may have been quoting Kafka, is both something we long for and something we dread. Thus, the double meaning of homesickness. Home is never home, we are always missing somewhere else, somewhere unrelated to the home we inhabit at the time of missing. Nostalgia, therefore, is a kind of fuel, a synapse enabler, returning us, like Odysseus, to the places we have willfully abandoned. Longing in this figuration is activated not by loss but by time itself, our own vanishing selves. But what of those wrenched out of time, not willfully, but violently? The Syrians, the Mexicans, the South Americans, the Somalians, the persecuted, the hunted, the tormented? Rachel?

THE END OF DESIRE

When my boyfriend described the last agonies of his aunt who died from emphysema, I was unmoved, but when I read that smoking causes wrinkles, I became motivated. That time quitting lasted several months, maybe even a year, but somewhere along the line I convinced myself that I should take it up again. It might have been the weight gain. It might have been the camaraderie—leaving a party and joining a small clutch of nicotine addicts in a corner of the backyard always seemed to me preferable to hanging around a table of sorrowful hors d'oeuvres. It was dark, we were together in a mostly silent, relaxing way.

It's true, as I've gotten older, I've become not only vainer, but less friendly, more willing to blow smoke between myself and another which I'm told signals troubles with intimacy. On the other hand, that small clutch of cigarette fiends offered me something—permission to pause (on the inhale and exhale) without seeming idiotic.

And I always liked the pose I believe I struck with cigarette in hand. Gazing through a swirl of smoke, as if intent on something profound. Without a cigarette, I have a lost, dumb look, as if I'd rather be elsewhere, watching TV.

Nevertheless, I finally threw my pack of Marlboro Lights into the trash. It was not a whole-hearted decision and left a crater in my psyche, like losing a best friend. She will never return. And if she briefly reappears in the backyard of some boring party, you'll find her repulsive and not worth the emotional investment.

MY BOYFRIEND'S SIGNIFICANT OTHERS

A wort hog head presiding over a wooden devil with an erection, a number of wind-up toys, a theremin, a photograph of sumo wrestlers, a photograph of Bettie Page (quite valuable), a couple of Samurai swords, an authentic bow and arrow, four African spears, a row of WWI helmets, a bust of Einstein, a human skull wearing his old cub scout hat, a human fetus skeleton in a bell jar, a minstrel marionette, painted red, bronzed baby shoes (his), a cast iron bank, a model of a vintage red MG, a model of a vintage black MG, a row of gun paintings (by me), a two-headed baby made of rubber, chattering teeth, an animatronic monkey with cymbals, a hand grenade, a Hitler skunk door stop from the 1940s, a Magic 8-Ball, a balalaika, a tambourine, a few wooden flutes, a Bambi doll and a dried snake.

MY BRILLIANT CAREER

When I was very old, I decided to become a jazz singer. I hired a pianist who bore with me as I struggled through the standards. I had memorized those standards as a kid, note for note: the *Ella Sings Rodgers and Hart* album and the *Ella Sings Gershwin* album and the Frank Sinatra *In the Wee Small Hours* album and the Anita O'Day album rereleased in 1962 called *This is Anita*. And more. This was my advantage—perhaps my only gift. I don't have a good "instrument," but I read that the voice improves with practice, even when the vocal chords are ancient. After a year, I'd expanded my range, but my pitch was often wobbly, my intonation annoying. I needed to think about breathing. Eventually I climbed on the stage with a group of musicians and sang "Detour Ahead," a rendition I stole from Jane Monheit. Was I any good? There was a scatter of polite applause. Someone told me I had spunk.

Next, I went on tour across the country. Nightly, I stepped on a big stage in front of thousands. I wore spangles and a crown. I called myself La Femme and my signature piece was "La Vie en Rose," a song my mother sang at cocktail parties. Her signature piece. I became very famous and someone wrote a book about me. After a while, I became bored with fame and the crowds annoyed me. I was always inebriated and lonely, plus I was no spring chicken. I hated the fans with their desperate fawnings, their crass demands for my autograph. When I shot myself on stage, it was front-page news around the world. Then I became a ghost, which was a better life.

TEETH

The past, which we distill down to its essential events, always seems simpler, truer and more well-meaning than the present. When Duncan Grant moved in with Vanessa and stayed on for 40 years, there was no ambiguity; it was clear he would do as he pleased; it was clear she'd suffer as women do, not being loved enough. We look back on them fondly, their suffering quaint and bearable from this perspective.

I lost my tooth on a piece of sushi, then today it was cemented back in by the dentist who assured me it would not last. Sooner or later many of my teeth would fall out and I would be forced into an implant or a partial, the latter referred to as an *appliance*, like a stove or a washing machine. How about wooden teeth, like George Washington? I quipped. The dentist shrugged, his plaid hoodie visible beneath his white coat. Don't talk, he said.

When Rachel calls from the nursing home she forgets I've seen her hours ago. When will you come home? she wonders. I am home. I never go away. I won't leave you.

The arc of my life has been pre-determined as if by a rocket launch. There was a time I was on my way up and at the very top took in the panoramic view of my expansive and lovely accomplishments-to-be. Here I am descending.

I've never given rockets a thought until now. Like cartoons careening through illustrations of sky, then exploding in jagged red and yellow lines, they are a good metaphor for a life span, I suppose. What wish do they fulfill? I wanted a ship to push onto a little lake. I wanted float, not roar not blast.

Duncan Grant painted post-impressionistic figures inclining toward fauvism since he often smeared faces with bright oranges, electric blues. He designed fabrics, one of which is of the west wind blowing long wavy black lines of wind; it could have been a rocket. A splotch of ice green speeding against a white background. He was unfaithful. But no one minded. As a young man he was incredibly beautiful.

The teeth have been a sad motif for me, a metaphor for my depressive intervals. Can I tell you the number of times I've discovered one in my mouth, rolling around like a lifesaver? There is not a dentist I don't disgust, who doesn't look at me with either pity or irritation. Of the two, I prefer the latter.

Rockets are of the future in our past stories of the future. Teeth are the story of a specific past as are Duncan Grant's fanciful fabrics. At the Charleston house in Sussex, the walls were painted by Duncan and Vanessa, swirls of blue and green, figures on door panels, coyly peeking out from behind. In those days, what of teeth? Rotted and brown, many missing, chipped, smiles behind hands. We should be grateful the story of teeth does not survive, being too disgusting for the historical sensibility, thus marring our nostalgia.

In the present, my daughter calls me. I'm here, I tell her. Always here here here. Who will remember this? I will, since I'm writing it down.

SECOND ARROW

I worry that my memory is tinged—indeed *ruled*—by a stalwart, victim narrative. When I began to meditate again, after having dropped the practice from my life for many years, my shallow, self-serving side bubbled up in all its splendor. I became mindfully aware. For example, my eyes are apt to fill with easy tears at the sight of an old woman with a shopping cart full of rags, yet I go cold at a row of tattooed rednecks outside the Circle K eating their candy bars. In a restaurant, I will note with disdain a table of ladies with Republican hair, and I am quick to take offense at a brusque retort from a waitperson. It drives me crazy when someone uses the wrong word and I have no sympathy for the drug addict, though I should since my own son is among their number. Other things, too numerous to mention—snobbery left over from a former life and in all cases markers of class: acrylic nails, big hair, country western music, romance novels, TV dinners, plastic-covered furniture, polyester anything, Jell-O molds and dogs wearing clothing. I am never not evaluating, categorizing, pronouncing smug, confident judgment. Except today, in the grocery store, a woman with dreads and a long, plaid, ruffled skirt gave me pause: Do I envy or pity her? Is she hip or homeless? And then it was hard to tell anything about anything.

WHAT HAS TO BE BROKEN BEFORE YOU USE IT? *

It is difficult for me to visit my daughter in her facility—to observe the white board with the day's riddle scrawled with marker, to make my way through the rows of wheelchaired invalids being fed by patient aides in white uniforms and orange aprons, to breathe in the air of the food carts with their metal hoods, barely disguising the boiled smell of vegetables and gray meat, commingling with the smell of shit and floral room deodorizer. As I approach her building (which looks so nice on the outside with its citrus grove and blue trim), I am never not imagining myself being repeatedly smashed over the head with a rock or kicked in the stomach by a booted enemy or just screaming until my head explodes—which is when I realize it is all imaginary, these dramas that rage inside me, in scenes, in passions I witness rather than experience, even though it is the witnessing that leaves me depleted, exhausted and impatient to leave.

*an egg

WELCOME

Today at Rachel's I am approached by a very tall woman wearing an ankle-length pink dress. It is trimmed with a band of faded orange and a little rickrack marches along the hem. She advances with ferocious deliberation, walking robot-wise, clump-clump across the vinyl tiled floor. Her face is filled with gray lines and sorrow, a road map of deep creases. Nevertheless, I think she is younger than she seems. She is upright as she clomps forth, and her large hands are smooth, her fingers long and bony. From a distance, her face seemed as if etched by tragedy, but now I see it has a muted joy that tug her features brightly upwards. Her eyes are blue, very blue chinks of light buried in her blanket of wrinkles and folds. Her hair straggly and yellow, a little gray happening. When she reaches me, she opens her arms and I fall into them. *Welcome*, she whispers, gripping me by the shoulders and pulling me into her tall and solid body, *Welcome* she keeps saying. She seems to be made of a severe, impervious material, and when I am clutched to her, it is like being clutched by a wall. *Welcome, oh welcome,* she says, this wall of woman, the soft webbing of her face beaming down on me, shrouding me in mistaken love.

THE BARGAIN

After she bunched up the trash in the front seat—Fed Ex envelope and bubble wrap and an ad for Cox cable—she turned off the car engine and sat there for a minute staring into space, trash still in hand. She would dump it in the big can by the door, then she would go through the doors to the Unit and press a bell. There was a lanky man in a white tee shirt sitting at one of the wrought iron tables in front and he said something to her, and she smiled. She hadn't heard him, but she smiled as if she did. Her life was being performed in *as ifs*. It was a valid approach. Getting up *as if* the day would be fine, and so on. Not that she really had anything to complain about, just a feeling of dread that permeated everything, then lifted. It was odd, the feeling of dread, its momentary intense habitation of her; she could feel the tears in the backs of her eyes, though, and that was something that indicated movement at least, a place to go. Yeats said that the "ancient, glittering eyes" of the Chinese figurines, though they beheld tragedy, were gay. Something of this sort she felt keeping her on the planet.

Of course, Yeats was talking about figurines. Had they broken down and wept it would have been a miracle.

The lanky man was sitting with his sister and later she discovered they had similar names: Dana and Diane. And the rest of us is called Dave, Dane and Debbie, he explained, but this was later when they were on their way out. At the moment, she passed him by and smiled, then crammed the trash into the can.

Since it was Sunday, no one much was around. No one at the front desk. She used the rest room for a minute, locked the door. The mirror contained her yellowish image. She flushed and the sound echoed loudly since it was a bigger room than necessary. Sink, toilet, an empty white can. It could have contained a bed. No window. A urine-colored box.

On the way to the Unit she passed a troop of wheelchair patients, some in motion, some sitting there slumped as was the usual posture of those in wheelchairs in this place. They could not seem to be erect. The lady with the helmet said something to her, perhaps it was, *are you Rachel's mother?* for the hundredth time. And she smiled and said *yes!* her voice sounding sprightly and insincere. She resisted engagement and felt bad about it. She hated the place and felt sorry for everyone.

There was a schedule scrawled on a white-board and already it had faded, as if having been scrawled with a worn-out marker. When she taught, she'd used those markers and often they wore out, necessitating a trip to the department for another marker, but since class was usually in progress, she had no time to go back. Before class, she could never seem to remember to check the adequacy of the marker, so after a while, students began to bring white-board markers to class.

This white board was nailed to the block wall in the hallway. She strained to read it, it listed activities and times. One such was "nail sculpting" and she wondered about that—was it like a manicure? It sounded fancy, like a spa treatment, but that was unlikely here. Anyway, nail sculpting seemed to have been scheduled for a Wednesday that had just passed. She made a mental note to ask Rachel about nail sculpting. Had she had her nails sculpted? This would make them laugh as turns of phrase amused them.

Someone let her into the Unit, so she didn't have to press the bell. The woman who let her in, an aide wearing a flowered uniform and white stockings, shielded the keypad carefully. One might just as easily memorize the beep sounds, she thought, having seen this in a movie. There was Rachel with a big blue bib around her neck sitting at a long table. Hardly anyone else around. She wondered if they all left with relatives on Sunday. Rachel's face always lit up when she saw her mother, as if she hadn't seen her for weeks or years. She usually swung her good arm to the left in her excitement. Macha!

Let's blow this popsicle stand—

I'm so happy to see you, just one hug and a kiss—

OK, but let's go eat something and don't pull my arm—

Sorry—

I love this new wheelchair, thank you very much, it's so great—

I like it too because it's light and I can get it into the trunk easily—

Outside she becomes aware of the pellucid day. "Pellucid" is a word she'd been intending to use in a sentence. It's almost as if you can see through the air in an infinite regression, like a series of mirrors placed at intervals in an otherwise small room. It was like looking into the unrecoverable past. A small breeze in the ornamental orange trees, which otherwise look hair-sprayed, moves them in a clump and underneath, in the long gray shifting shadows, the man in his white tee and his sister sit on the wrought iron chairs. The man is stretched out almost horizontal, his feet in front of him and flexed at the ankles. Foreshortened. If she were to draw him, his feet, crossed at the ankles in green sport shoes with black waffled rubber soles, would be twice as large as his head.

Hello! says Rachel. You look so comfortable!

Hello, Rachel, says the man who turns out to be called Dana.

It is hard to tell which of these—Dana or his sister Diane—is the resident. She seems to be wearing a number of mismatched items all topped with a patterned scarf, but it was impolite to take too careful note of these.

Then Rachel and her mother open the gate and push down an incline to the door of the car. The gate is heavy, and the daughter has to hold it open with her one good hand. The mother helps with the hand that is not gripping the handle of the chair. The incline is steep for a wheelchair. There must be an ADA rule being broken. The mother's arthritis in her thumb is throbbing from holding onto the chair handle with one hand. If she were to let go, the daughter would careen down the incline and fall over. The mother is wearing a brown skirt that she bought at a thrift store for a dollar.

Guess how much this cost?

I have no idea—where did you get it?

That would give it away, you just have to guess.

I would say about $40.

No! Much, much less!

NEW NAMES FOR ME

In old age I have acquired a new name: Mimi. It is my "grandmother name" and my daughter chose it for me. My first grandson, at three, had been calling me Mock, a name that I had grown used to, but my daughter disapproved. No, you will be Mimi, she decreed. So it has been Mimi for some years now and I am happy enough with that name, though it lacks the ironic edge of Mock.

My sugar-loving granddaughter, Hannah, calls me Meemaw. I love this name. It makes me think of a cartoon character by Al Capp. In response I call her Heehaw, and I picture the two of us, Meemaw and Heehaw, Age and Beauty, skipping down a dusty road with a picnic of candy in our checkered knapsacks.

I am drawn to the name Haddock and from now on would appreciate it if family and friends would call me Haddock. Everyone laughs at this. Most likely, Haddock subconsciously appeals because it rhymes with Mock and thus retains the ironic edge I seem to subconsciously yearn for.

Nevertheless, I remain Mimi to my grandchildren and even to my children and my children's and grandchildren's friends. Mimi—a waspy, fussily coiffed grandma who watches daytime TV—a name that almost describes me.

WHO WILL REPLACE GABY HOFFMANN?

I lost a tooth and it was cemented back. The nurse—Monica—scraped out the remnants of cement from under the gumline. The gumline beneath which that little piece of rice from a salmon nigiri dislodged my tooth. That tooth is on its way out, is how the dentist puts it. Maybe a week, maybe a year. The past, as remembered, does not decay, which is why such reality will outlast us, framed for eternity.

~

William Wyler's film *Dead End* features Humphrey Bogart who dies before half the film is over and Claire Trevor who has a bit part as a prostitute. It's New York City in the 30s. The city assembled on a Hollywood lot is strangely beautiful, familiar. Sometimes other people's history feels personal, like a loss of one's own.

~

In a certain daytime television show a group of women sit around and discuss current events. Because the topics are often controversial and political, the producers have made sure that the women are diverse—liberal and conservative, black and white, a balance so exquisitely maintained that when one of the women leaves the show, the others feel unable to continue without her.

PROPERTY

My beautiful mesquite is plaguing my neighbor—it reaches into her yard—and drops its stuff onto her property. Little yellow flowers that make golden islands in her pool. To me, very beautiful. Tiny leaves that clog the pool drain. The roots are pushing up the patio brick. The return of the repressed, Freud would say. She doesn't care for my front yard oleander either. She has her gardener chop off the part on her side. Her land is covered with pink pebbles and, in every season, her front yard has Christmas lights wrapped around its single cactus, a saguaro that I suppose is stately, but on its own like this, in a sea of glistening pink, it looks artificial, as if camouflaging a cell phone tower.

Once she told me my oleander was "blocking her air flow," as well as preventing her from seeing encroaching intruders. She has the story of a woman who was raped behind a wall.

But she herself has erected a tall wall separating our backyards because she believes certain walls are necessary—such as the capital w Wall an hour south of us and guarded by border patrol to keep out the drug addicts, terrorists, murderers and brown people. In this, too, we are sharply, angrily, achingly divided.

FORT DA

This is the story: The child hurls a toy from his playpen, a cookie from her highchair tray. A Freudian game, practicing the return of the mother. The child cries; the mother retrieves the object. In this sense, suffering (loss) is the condition for the acutest joy (redemption). I conclude that Chris who suffers in prison, again and again banishing himself from our lives, is waiting for me to reclaim him. And over and over I fail to do so.

Once, driving along, he said to me, *You always know how to make me feel better, Mom*. He must have been about 12, a shy kid, sandy-haired, he didn't reach his full height until much later. We had been going to a department store to buy him shoes. I was poor at the time. We even charged dinners at the department store.

Now he writes me letters. *I worry I will never see you again, Mom. I don't think I could cope.*

LAST WORKSHOP

We are gathered in the dark green living room of my Salt Lake City home. It's snowing hard outside. The students are kicking off their boots in the entry or, politely, the front stoop, draping their Patagonias over the bannister, gloves and scarves and hats on the hall floor in a heap.

They bring wine and treats, most notably Oreos which they know I can't resist. This is Graduate Fiction, 600-something-something, and it is around 2010. I am living in an 1896 Victorian with ancient fir floors and a vintage electric fireplace that spews blue gas flames and heat. We have just read James Salter's "Am Strande von Tanger" and I am pontificating about the opening sentences: *Barcelona at dawn. The hotels are dark. All the great avenues are pointing to the sea.*

With those melancholic, lyrical sentences, I say, we are set on a course of heartbreak and enlightenment. I am on my fifth Oreo.

But nothing actually happens, someone says. And someone else says, that's what's so amazing, it's just a day trip with friends. It's all in the undertones. And another says, I don't get why at the end there is no clear resolution. It feels unfinished.

I am on my eighth Oreo.

She is smarter than he is, he is too easily seduced by their friend. He is shallow. No wonder she turns away from him at the end.

But he isn't really seduced. It's all innuendo. It happens all the time. A little blip in the relationship is all, from which everyone moves on.

Is that what happens?

And what about the bird, the dead bird? Is that not a symbol slapping us in the face?

It has a wonderful mood. Are all his stories like that?

Does she stay with him is what I'm wondering—

How are we supposed to feel about the ending? On the one hand it's good that she realizes he's a jerk, letting their parrot die as well as obviously becoming enchanted by her stupid friend; on the other hand, what's she supposed to do now, she married the guy. Poor Nico.

I say, someone take these Oreos away from me.

Someone says, no one likes a happy ending.

Someone else says, right. That's all the cookies we get.

POSITIVITY

And you are? The woman behind the ticket counter examines me with misgiving, but this is the airport, where suspicion is part of the job description.

It's getting late. I like to be at the gate when they arrive otherwise, in my imagination, they will run all over the place, get lost and ultimately kidnapped. Grandmother, I say, and she breaks into the beatific smile reserved for grandmothers. She is wearing very dark lipstick and her name is Pam. Aw. I can't wait for mine. Her eyes mist. Will they spend the holidays with you? Yes. What about their parents? Don't their parents want them? No. That's so odd, she says, looking away. Do you see a lot of them? Yes. What are their names? Jesus, I say, audibly. She gives me a hurt look.

I have two minutes before touchdown. She shuffles papers, enters things on her computer, shuffles more papers, excuses herself to go ask someone something.

Finally, she is back with my gate pass fluttering in her hand. She repeats some instructions to me twice and loudly, now that she knows I'm a grandmother. She will not release the pass until I acknowledge that I understand, and even then, she teases me with it, extending and withdrawing her hand. You don't have to snatch, she chides.

At the gate the children rush to me, crashing into my knees and arms. No kidnappers in sight. Pam, now presiding at the gate, is coming at us with a number of forms to be signed. Happy New Year! she says brightly, since it is around that time. Try to be a little more positive.

PARALLEL STATES OF LOSS

I have been unable to reach Fianna since the first day when she came to play with the girls.

That day, after she so charmingly imitated a unicorn, I walked her home and when we rang the doorbell which was situated next to a plaque which said *Doll Repair*, it was answered by a very tall woman who was wiping her hands on a square apron, her face encased in shadow.

In the gloom of the living room, the heads of many dolls stared forlornly into space—as if lit from within, all of their movable eyelids were wide open. From here we could see their slightly moth-eaten eyelashes and the frills of their costumes which entailed lace at the neck.

Here is Fianna, I said to the woman. We have brought her home.

After that we never saw Fianna. I would say it was the last time we saw Fianna, but of course I am hoping there will be more Fianna sightings even though the girls no longer require her presence.

The girls are gone. For a short time, they were here in my world occupying my sofa, demanding their special cups and now, nothing.

Fianna is also gone, and I cannot help but note a pleasing parallel in this state of affairs, these two disconcerting absences.

THE GREAT WATER

We beheld what was ours. Undulant land
Rose layer by layer till at last the sea
Far away flashed. W. H. Auden

The I-Ching advises whether it furthers one to cross the great water or not, meaning should the consultee proceed with whatever it is, or stay put. Woolf once said that writing a novel was like dragging a blurred shape across a body of water. The closer it came, the clearer it got. That's a paraphrase. It was the River Ouse she walked into, stones in her pockets, not waiting for clarity.

That river is in Sussex, a county, like most of rural England, spattered with beautiful hazy fields which at dusk swarm with the soft white blurred forms of sheep and small farmhouses. Compared to our countrysides, especially the countryside in the southwest, which is tan desert space littered with the spokes of cactus, Sussex is composed of curves and shades of subtle variated greens, a landscape that does not accommodate great contrasts in light. Beneath cloudless skies, the desert light is harder and the shadows at dusk lay flat and dark and the angular mountains in the background, indifferent, by which I think I mean that the mountains seem unconnected to the fate of the desert, even though—technically—they are of the desert.

I had not intended on writing about landscape or even Woolf who suicided perhaps because of the war—some say this, anyway. I imagine she just gave up, felt she had done enough, felt there was nothing left to do. Some of us believe that we must do things continually to prove ourselves worthy of life. A TV character, explaining his depression, said he had used up his store of happiness—that we were each allotted a certain amount and that his was at an end.

This is what my favorite guru says: Keep in mind that you are a spirit experiencing a human life. My guru who exists in a podcast.

I have a friend who's cultivated her neighborhood rabbits. Her three favorites she calls Simon, Schuster and Lake. They have grown quite fat, nestling together under a creosote bush in her yard. At daybreak, I talk to a particular mourning dove, a sweet gray woman inhabiting a branch of the mesquite. Hello Darling, I say, and she answers, a beautiful two-toned sentence. Spirit to spirit.

Centuries of English literature have not prepared us for the desert, the mesquite's sprawl, the sweet mourning doves, the unfriendly agave, now sprouting a gray-green frond as tall as the house. Soon—I give it a month—it will topple, wrecking my driveway tarp.

Our attention acclimates as our bodies do—yawning space for the glitter of foliage. Silence for the din of soft hills.

Living here, we learn something about difficulty. The sun is merciless, water is scarce, cacti pierce the skin, shade is respite and balm.

Who would not be drawn to Sussex with its green and sheep, where the sky is lower, cozier, where my hero, nonetheless, found life unbearable? It was during the time they were bombing London, when fire rained from the Constable clouds and extinguished everything from history to geography.

Have we humans used up our stores of happiness and good luck? We spirits posing as humans and doing a crap job?

In the desert, there is no Great Water in sight. We invent our seductions and grow into them; in the same way a baby saguaro is protected by a palo verde (called a "nurse tree"), we finally accommodate and evolve. One cannot help but be wooed by light, rabbits, bird-gongs, parcels of green and gold, the jutting-up things that look like giant penises. Even my swimming pool blueness, sky therein contained like a painting of sky. Our little lives rounded in a sleep, as if this were not all along a dream.

Outside a bird is flapping around in the mesquite. He comes and goes when he feels like it. The world is thin and smudged, a rustling veil behind which a million billion sultans dance.

The sea, far away, flashes.

THE FUTURE

We have our inheritance. We have our IRA investments. We have initiated our phased retirement. In front of us, the longed-for perspective—a wide path narrowing, then vanishing over the horizon. Who knows how long we will travel this path before we get, to complicate the metaphor, felled by a tree or a wayward bullet. Nonetheless, it is all in order, the investments, the bank accounts, the dizzying idea of freedom.

Although the dizzying idea of freedom gives us pause. Perhaps, when we were younger, we'd have been able to contemplate such a state of mind without feeling dizzy, that is to say, unfocused and even a little hard of hearing. The dizzying idea of *what*? And yet freedom is a word we've heard all our lives, why now are we suddenly deaf? Are we so typical that the dizzying idea of F is terrifying? Where are we without our students, our alarm clock, our workplace complaints? Or rather: who are we?

We are she who will climb on that road, in all its pale gray dullness, and march.

Notes:

"Television"
The neighbor's TV was probably a 1946 RCA 630TS, a sleeker and less elaborate 10" than what exists in my memory.

"Polio"
My mother's polio occurred right before the outbreak in 1949 and a month or so after my brother Billy was taken away to Grasslands' hospital. My sister and I caught the virus but were spared the worst effects.

"After Lacan"
Refers to Lacan's famous *stade du miroir*—mirror stage—the empowering moment when an infant recognizes her own reflection in the mirror and initiates her sense of self.

"Miltown"
Meprobamate, a minor tranquilizer, also known as "mother's little helper," was popular with 50s housewives.

"Bam Zoom"
In *The Honeymooners* (1955-1978), Jackie Gleason played Ralph, the aggrieved, bombastic husband of the unflappable Alice, played by Audrey Meadows. *Bam Zoom* was Ralph's mantra, usually bellowed.

"Allegory"
The last lines refer to "The First Elegy" in Rilke's *Duino Elegies*: "Who, if I cried out, would hear me among the Angelic / Orders?"

"Happy Days"
Roz Kelly played Pinky Tuscadero, the Fonz's girlfriend, famous for her white boots and motorcycle. I longed to be her, but I lacked style.

"Notes from a Voyage"
The SS Constitution was one of the great ocean liners in the days before ocean liners were demoted to cruise ships. The Constitution was famous for transporting Grace Kelly and her entourage to her wedding in 1956, and hosting an episode of *I Love Lucy*. My actual journal from 1960, a red leather-bound book, my monogram stamped in gold, is filled with lackluster information of the sort in "Voyage" and more than a few malapropisms.

"Coming of Age"
The Azalea Festival changed its name to the Norfolk NATO Festival in 2009.

"Jackpot"
"Calvino's Baron" is a reference to Italo Calvino's 1957 novel, *The Baron in the Trees.*

"Panic"
"As I have seen a swan with bootless labour . . . " (Henry VI. 1.4.) Shakespeare. "Bootless cries" (Sonnet 29) Ibid.

"Rosa"
CETA (The Comprehensive Training and Employment Act), whose purpose was to provide jobs and training for workers in the public sector, was signed into law in 1973 by Richard Nixon.

"Typewriter"
The old Underwoods sell for over $1,000 these days. Too bad I lost mine.

"Nostos"
A Greek word meaning returning home after a sea voyage (cf. Homer's *Odyssey*, Joyce's *Ulysses*). I rely here on the implication of longing for home or longing to return home (as in "nostalgia").

"The Bargain"
The Yeats poem referenced is "Lapis Lazuli."

"Who Will Replace Gaby Hoffmann?"
The TV show referred to is, of course, *The View*.

"*Fort Da*"
The notion that the child in the Freudian game is schooled to suffering as a preamble to satisfaction is a paraphrase of an interpretation I borrow from Rachel Cusk's novel *Outline*.

"The Great Water"
The Auden quotation is from *The Age of Anxiety*. "Our little lives rounded in a sleep" is an appropriation of Shakespeare's words in *The Tempest*: "We are such stuff / as dreams are made on; and our little life / is rounded with a sleep."

Acknowledgments:

I'm grateful to the editors of the following journals in which some of these pieces have appeared:

The Collagist: "Shame," "Gurus," "C'est Moi"
Seneca Review: "Polio," "My First Husband" as "A Memoir," "War" (as "1965"), "Poet," "Compulsion," "Touch"
Ocean State Review: "Allegory," "School," "Shoe," "Mirror"

And I'm beyond thankful for my wonderful editor Martha Rhodes, her assistant, and Four Way intern, Spencer Williams, and Jonathan Blunk, whose careful edits and suggestions made this a much better book; and for all the Four Way staff, especially director, Ryan Murphy, for his brilliant book design.

And many thanks to my good friends, Cynthia Hogue, David Shields, Debra Spark, and Zita Ingham for reading earlier drafts and encouraging me onward. And to the love of my life, Steve Romaniello, for all the important stuff.

Karen Brennan is the author of fiction, poetry, and nonfiction. A recipient of a National Endowment for the Arts fellowship and an AWP award, she is Professor Emerita of English and Creative Writing for the University of Utah. Her stories, poems, and essays have been included in anthologies from Norton, Penguin, Graywolf, Georgia, and Michigan, among others. Since 1991, she has served as core faculty in the Warren Wilson MFA Program for Writers. *Television, a memoir* is her eighth book.

Publication of this book was made possible by grants and donations. We are also grateful to those individuals who participated in our 2021 Build a Book Program. They are:

Anonymous (16), Maggie Anderson, Susan Kay Anderson, Kristina Andersson, Kate Angus, Kathy Aponick, Sarah Audsley, Jean Ball, Sally Ball, Clayre Benzadón, Greg Blaine, Laurel Blossom, Adam Bohannon, Betsy Bonner, Lee Briccetti, Joan Bright, Jane Martha Brox, Susan Buttenwieser, Anthony Cappo, Carla and Steven Carlson, Paul and Brandy Carlson, Renee Carlson, Alice Christian, Karen Rhodes Clarke, Mari Coates, Jane Cooper, Ellen Cosgrove, Peter Coyote, Robin Davidson, Kwame Dawes, Michael Anna de Armas, Brian Komei Dempster, Renko and Stuart Dempster, Matthew DeNichilo, Rosalynde Vas Dias, Kent Dixon, Patrick Donnelly, Lynn Emanuel, Blas Falconer, Elliot Figman, Jennifer Franklin, Helen Fremont and Donna Thagard, Gabriel Fried, John Gallaher, Reginald Gibbons, Jason Gifford, Jean and Jay Glassman, Dorothy Tapper Goldman, Sarah Gorham and Jeffrey Skinner, Lauri Grossman, Julia Guez, Sarah Gund, Naomi Guttman and Jonathan Mead, Kimiko Hahn, Mary Stewart Hammond, Beth Harrison, Jeffrey Harrison, Melanie S. Hatter, Tom Healy and Fred Hochberg, K.T. Herr, Karen Hildebrand, Joel Hinman, Deming Holleran, Lillian Howan, Thomas and Autumn Howard, Catherine Hoyser, Elizabeth Jackson, Jessica Jacobs and Nickole Brown, Christopher Johanson, Jen Just, Maeve Kinkead, Alexandra Knox, Lindsay and John Landes, Suzanne Langlois, Laura Lauth, Sydney Lea, David Lee and Jamila Trindle, Rodney Terich Leonard, Jen Levitt, Howard Levy, Owen Lewis, Matthew Lippman, Jennifer Litt, Karen Llagas, Sara London and Dean Albarelli, Clarissa Long, James Longenbach, Cynthia Lowen, Ralph and Mary Ann Lowen, Ricardo Maldonado, Myra Malkin, Jacquelyn Malone, Carrie Mar, Kathleen McCoy, Ellen McCulloch-Lovell, Lupe Mendez, David Miller, Josephine Miller, Nicki Moore, Guna Mundheim, Matthew Murphy and Maura Rockcastle, Michael and Nancy Murphy, Myra Natter, Jay Baron Nicorvo, Ashley Nissler, Kimberly Nunes, Rebecca and Daniel Okrent, Robert Oldshue and Nina Calabresi, Kathleen Ossip, Judith Pacht, Cathy McArthur Palermo, Marcia and Chris Pelletiere,

Sam Perkins, Susan Peters and Morgan Driscoll, Patrick Phillips, Robert Pinsky, Megan Pinto, Connie Post, Kyle Potvin, Grace Prasad, Kevin Prufer, Alicia Jo Rabins, Anna Duke Reach, Victoria Redel, Martha Rhodes, Paula Rhodes, Louise Riemer, Sarah Santner, Amy Schiffman, Peter and Jill Schireson, Roni and Richard Schotter, James and Nancy Shalek, Soraya Shalforoosh, Peggy Shinner, Anita Soos, Donna Spruijt-Metz, Ann F. Stanford, Arlene Stang, Page Hill Starzinger, Marina Stuart, Yerra Sugarman, Marjorie and Lew Tesser, Eleanor Thomas, Tom Thompson and Miranda Field, James Tjoa, Ellen Bryant Voigt, Connie Voisine, Moira Walsh, Ellen Dore Watson, Calvin Wei, John Wender, Eleanor Wilner, Mary Wolf, and Pamela and Kelly Yenser.